Sex or Symbol

EROTIC IMAGES
OF GREECE AND ROME

Sex or Symbol

EROTIC IMAGES
OF GREECE AND ROME

CATHERINE JOHNS

A COLONNADE BOOK
Published by British Museum Publications

Colonnade Books
are published by British Museum
Publications Ltd and are offered as
contributions to the enjoyment, study and
understanding of art, archaeology and
history

The same publishers also produce the
official publications of the British Museum

Published by British Museum Publications Ltd
46 Bloomsbury Street, London WC1B 3QQ

British Library Cataloguing in Publication Data
Johns, Catherine
    Sex or symbol: erotic images of Greece
    and Rome. – (A Colonnade book)
    1. Erotic art – Greece   2. Erotic art –
    Rome
    I. Title
    704.9′428′0938   N8217.E6
    ISBN 0-7141-8042-4

Designed by Roger Davies

Set in Photina
and Printed in Great Britain by
Balding and Mansell,
London and Wisbech

Note on the spelling of Greek and Latin words

Even a work as authoritative as the *Oxford
Classical Dictionary* admits that it is virtually
impossible to be consistent in the transliteration
of Greek words: many of them are familiar in
Latin or anglicised versions, while even Latin
names are often known to the reader in English
spellings which have been used for centuries,
and therefore look very strange if the original
forms are used. As this book deals with both
Greek and Roman culture, there is no case to be
made for a pedantic approach to Greek words
where more familiar Latin spellings exist (e.g.
Bacchus rather than Bakkhos), and I have
therefore simply used the forms which come
most naturally to me, whether Greek, Latin or
purely English. I have placed the word 'phallus'
in the latter category, and have consequently
preferred the English plural 'phalluses' to the
Latin *phalli*; the original Greek form is *phallos*,
plural *phalloi*.

The references in the text to illustrations in
black and white are in normal type: those in
italic type refer to colour illustrations.

Contents

Scene of a couple from the inside of a red-figure cup. The atmosphere of this scene contrasts strongly with that on the outside of the cup (see 107).

Acknowledgements

In late 1977 the undergraduates in the Archaeology Society at Exeter University invited me to give a lecture; from the subjects I suggested to them, they selected, to my surprise, 'Erotic Art of Greece and Rome'. My first acknowledgement is therefore to them, for the impetus to organise the material into the form which has ultimately resulted in this book. The questions and comments of both lecturers and students of Archaeology and Classics at Exeter and at the other Universities (Cardiff, Leeds, Reading, Southampton and London) where I have given the same paper have contributed greatly to my thinking on the subject.

I have had the benefit of discussions with several friends and colleagues on various aspects of the theme, but there are four in particular to whom I am especially grateful. Foremost amongst them is Tim Potter, who read the text in draft and made numerous detailed and constructive comments and criticisms. The typescript was also read by Val Rigby, Patsy Vanags and Elaine Paintin, all of whom made very perceptive suggestions and criticisms. I am deeply indebted to them. I should also like to thank David Wilson, the Director of the British Museum, for his encouragement, and Celia Clear and Jenny Chattington for their skill, practical help and sheer hard work.

The goodwill of the institutions which provided illustrations for the book was essential, and I have expressed my gratitude to them elsewhere, but I should also like to record my thanks personally to David Brown, Hugh Chapman, Geoff Marsh, Paul Arthur and Philip Kenrick for help in obtaining photographs. Beryl Bailey went to some trouble to seek out an obscure piece of information for me, and I should like to express my thanks to her also.

My greatest debt of all, for information, discussion, criticism and patient encouragement, is to Don Bailey; his contribution is immeasurable, and I acknowledge it in the only way possible, by dedicating the book to him.

Introduction

A great many cultures, past and present, have produced art which makes use of sexual motifs. The significance of such material is very wide ranging, and by no means all of it was made for the purpose of sexual titillation, which is at least partially implied by the term 'erotic'. In the recent past, particularly in the nineteenth century, all objects from ancient cultures which were shaped or decorated in a way that was considered improper by the very severe standards of the time were relegated to the category 'obscene'; if they were of sufficient artistic merit or archaeological importance to be housed in a museum, they were locked away in special collections which were made as difficult of access as possible. Only the most dedicated scholars and collectors could succeed in studying them, and even their motives were regarded as more than a little suspect. The layman interested in an ancient culture as a whole would find, at the most, oblique references to material of this kind in the general books available to him. Indeed, as we shall see, in the middle of the nineteenth century even serious scholarly work on this sensitive subject could be published only through publishers and booksellers who normally dealt in pornography.

The strict segregation of 'erotic' objects in museums has started to break down, though it is not yet complete and difficulties are still sometimes placed in the way of those who wish to study them. Even among scholarly circles there is still a tendency to study material of this kind in isolation rather than treating it as one of the many aspects of the culture which created it. There is no doubt that for a great many people the whole subject still holds a shock-value which belies our declared tolerance and open-mindedness in the late twentieth century and is a clear indication that reactions are less objective and more emotional than is consistent with sound scholarship. Even the increasing integration of the study of so-called erotica into archaeology and art-history still leaves the subject a long way behind other less sensitive ones, simply because there is so much leeway to make up. Deliberate suppression and segregation of this material in the previous century has distorted the picture, and it will take some time to restore the balance.

The disciplines of anthropology and psychology, which like history, archaeology and the study of art deal essentially with the nature and behaviour of people, developed somewhat later than archaeology, and were always seen as more scientific: the Victorian attitudes were beginning to waver a little, and it was possible for the relevance of sexuality and eroticism to these studies to be established and accepted very early on. It is now well known that sexual customs and conventions vary widely between different cultures, and what appears commonplace to one may be deeply offensive to another, and that in general this area of human behaviour is a particularly interesting and significant cultural indicator.

My aim in the chapters which follow is to illustrate some of the many examples of sexual imagery in the art of the classical cultures of Greece and Rome, to organise this material into broad categories according to its purpose and significance in antiquity, and to draw some inferences from it about those societies.

The geographical and chronological range I shall cover is very large, extending from Athens of the sixth century BC to the Roman Empire of the late fourth and early fifth centuries AD. Though there are undoubtedly great cultural differences at these extremes, there are also very basic similarities, above all in religious beliefs. The fact that the late-Roman Empire was officially Christian does not

Detail of a red-figure cup by the Triptolemos Painter showing a lovemaking scene (see 105). c.470 BC

mean that the underlying beliefs and practices of classical paganism had disappeared. It is these similarities which make it possible to trace links in the artistic imagery, which is very often concerned, however peripherally, with religious and related themes. The archaeological and artistic evidence offered may appear somewhat unbalanced: for example, the reader will notice that a very high proportion of the 'erotic' art illustrated from Greece occurs on painted Attic pottery of the sixth to fourth centuries BC, and that decorated ceramics in fact form a significant part of the evidence throughout. This is largely because pottery survives extremely well compared with other materials and will, therefore, always be one of our prime sources of information.

Of the three main categories into which I shall divide the material, two are essentially religious, while the third is more truly erotic. The variety of gods and goddesses worshipped in the Greek and Roman world included a great many who had some connection with the basic need to ensure and promote fertility, and it is natural that the visual imagery surrounding them, as well as some of the actual rituals involved in their worship, included phallic elements. The cult of Dionysos in particular gave rise not only to a widespread orgiastic cult, reaching from classical Greece into Christian Imperial Rome, but also provided the source of Greek drama (and, ultimately, of all European drama), which originally contained sexual elements linking it to the abandoned revels through which the god was honoured.

Phallic symbolism plays a very important role in the religious and superstitious beliefs of antiquity: because of its connection with the fortune-bringing fertility cults, the phallus becomes one of the most frequent and trusted good-luck charms of Greek and Roman culture. Phallic amulets were very common, especially in the Roman period and their wearers would not have thought of their connection with sexuality any more than most of us would consider the Christian implications of 'keeping our fingers crossed' against bad luck.

A considerable proportion of the apparently erotic images in Greek and Roman art can therefore be seen to be in some sense religious in aim. The very existence of these affected the attitude to the remaining category of objects intended to be sexually attractive and stimulating. Both Greek and Roman artefacts include many representations of lovemaking which seem to have no hidden meaning or purpose, but simply depict an enjoyable activity in a straightforward manner.

As we shall see, in sexually inhibited cultures such as that of nineteenth-century Britain, where sex was regarded as shameful, any object which might be thought to inflame sexual feeling was classified as erotic and therefore obscene, and its public display as deeply offensive. But neither the illustrations which depict deities concerned with fertility or the rituals used in their cults, nor the simple good-luck amulets which take the form of phallic or other sexual symbols, should be thought of as genuinely erotic. They were not intended to refer to sexual love nor to arouse sexual feeling. They seemed obscene to Victorian observers only because the repressive attitude to sexuality at that period made an astonishingly wide range of images appear erotically exciting: clearly a culture which can find the undraped legs of an inanimate object improper is going to be extremely disturbed by a model of the male genitalia, made for any purpose whatever. But phallic amulets were made for ancient Romans, not for Victorian Englishmen, and the latter failed in their duty as scholars when they suppressed such material because of their own prejudices. In studying cultures other than our own, whether ancient or contemporary, we have to try to set aside our cultural conditioning and assumptions, or we run the risk of reading into the material remains of those cultures meanings which were not intended or perceived by the people who made and used the objects. To classify such a wide variety of objects under the one heading of 'obscene' obscures some fundamental aspects of the culture we are studying and makes it impossible for us to gain a really deep understanding of that society.

We need, in fact, to ask ourselves whether the 'obscene' images, which appear to be very common in Greek and Roman art, were intended to shock and disgust those who used the objects on which they appear, whether they were intended to be sexually stimulating, or whether they may have had some other meaning which to us is not normally associated with overtly sexual images at all. The answer is that the different classes of sexual representation had a wide range of meanings, and that *none* of them, in antiquity, would have aroused the furtive, guilty and hostile response which they have *all* been accorded in the recent past. We have not yet freed ourselves from the prejudices of our recent past, and it is still extremely difficult for us to appreciate the truly erotic images in the matter-of-fact way which would best reflect their impact in antiquity, but we should make the effort because of their intrinsic interest and because of the way in which they can illuminate aspects of ancient life and society. Certainly they constitute a class of material which no serious student of the past can have any excuse at all for ignoring or suppressing.

In addition to the information we can gain about classical antiquity from the study of the sexual element in Greek and Roman art, we can acquire insights into the development of the discipline of archaeology, the strength and nature of the puritanical elements in nineteenth-century society, and the changing attitudes to the study of the past in general. Because of the very strong feelings aroused by 'obscene' material, the way in which it has been treated illustrates these fascinating themes more vividly than any other class of artefact. The treatment of erotic, and related, art is a barometer of the extent to which personal prejudice has risen and fallen in relation to scholarly integrity.

I
Collectors
and prudes

1 Avenue of Priapus on the island of
Delos, with columns carved as stone
phalluses. 3rd century BC

Cultivated Europeans have taken an interest in classical antiquities since the Renaissance, but the eighteenth and nineteenth centuries witnessed a great upsurge of activity in the study and collecting of such material. The scholars and rich dilettanti of that period started to form the basis of the modern discipline of archaeology, and at the same time their benefactions to museums laid the foundations of the major public collections. It is an unfortunate coincidence that this same era saw the rapid development of a refinement in speech and manners which eventually became sheer prudery, and even led on occasion to the most regrettable and unscholarly hypocrisy.

It will become clear in later chapters that it is impossible to study either classical antiquities or classical literature without encountering material which is of a forthrightly sexual nature. The changing manners of the late eighteenth century onwards are therefore important and relevant in any consideration of the history of archaeology. It is extremely difficult to chronicle the developing fear and hatred of so-called obscenity with any accuracy; trends, by their very nature, are constantly changing, and causes and effects can prove almost impossible to disentangle. At any given moment there will be examples to confirm an overall trend, and others which will seem to deny it; there will be moderns, in the van of progress, and diehard conservatives clinging to old ways. Furthermore, at the very time when a particular social attitude seems most firmly entrenched its strictures will have become so unbearable to some that there will probably be an underground movement running counter to it. In the case of sexual prudery, the middle of the nineteenth century was probably this point, and true to form, along with the counter-culture of pornography, there was also some serious study of subjects which for decades had been considered too gross to mention. It is important to note, firstly, that the movement towards 'purity' in speech, writing, the visual arts and entertainment was not concerned solely with sexual matters, but was a very wide-ranging attitude and, secondly, that though its heyday was in Victorian times, it was not a Victorian creation. It was already very well developed by the last two decades of the eighteenth century, a generation before Queen Victoria was born.

Throughout the 1700s notions of 'delicacy' and 'sensibility' as desirable attributes, especially in the female sex, steadily gained ground. There really was a time, hard to imagine for those of us still experiencing the reversal of this trend, when young people deplored the forthright manner and language, and even the behaviour, of their elders. The English language was changing very markedly, the pithy directness of the previous century being superseded by an increasingly formal, elegant and polysyllabic style, which was at the same time more 'refined' and euphemistic than seventeenth-century English. Though there are examples of increasing nervousness about visually improper material quite early in the eighteenth century, the tendency to expurgate or purify literature first becomes noticeable in the 1780s. Earlier examples of the practice (vividly, but to Victorian ears quite shockingly, referred to as the 'gelding' or 'castrating' of a text) had been too sporadic to constitute a real trend.

The basis for this kind of censorship and the reason for it are very complex: most people are guilty of a form of expurgation when reading to themselves, namely 'skipping the boring bits', and some forms of expurgation are indeed no more than that. Very often special editions for children will either shorten or simplify a text, or both, in order to hold the attention of a young reader better, and provided it is

2 Red-figure wine-cooler (*psykter*) by the vase-painter Douris, decorated with a scene of revelling satyrs. This is a print from an expurgated negative, in which the phallus of the central satyr has been painted out (see colour illustration, 3). 500–470 BC

1 *right* The god Pan and a she-goat. This small marble group from Herculaneaum is a classic of erotic art. 1st century BC

definitely stated that the text is an abridgement there is no harm in this at all. The editor has to decide what he believes to be essential and what dispensible; any such work is an implicit criticism of the original text, but if it leads a reader eventually to the original, it may well be justifiable. In preparing standard literature, such as the Bible and Shakespeare, for young people in this way, it is hardly surprising that some of the material which is most likely to be jettisoned is the wealth of sexual allusion to be found in both. Thus are the seeds of real expurgation sown, in which the editor removes all the author's words and ideas which he regards as improper, profane, or otherwise 'indelicate'. In due course a point is reached where such doctored texts are regarded as superior to the original and the extent, or even the very existence, of the gelding is no longer mentioned or admitted.

Even today many people believe that children should be shielded from all mention of sexual matters. This feeling is the last vestige of the concept of delicacy which took root in the late eighteenth century and grew until it engulfed society like a smothering ivy in the mid-nineteenth century. This concept of 'delicacy' becomes almost incomprehensible when it is closely examined. Women, initially young women but later all respectable women, even if they were grandmothers, were expected to display the utmost confusion and embarrassment at any sign of coarseness. Weeping, blushing and even swooning were in order: this demonstrated the extreme purity and innocence of their own characters. It was never explained how a genuinely innocent person could recognise that what he or she saw or heard was improper – a theory seems to have developed that the truly pure had a kind of sixth sense for this purpose. The unfortunate Robert Browning demonstrated later in the nineteenth century that the innocent are not always blessed with this useful instinct, by including in his poem *Pippa Passes* a highly improper word which everyone was too polite, too embarrassed, or possibly too ignorant themselves, to point out to him. Exposure to impropriety was held to coarsen the fibre irrevocably, and consequently it became necessary to protect the would-be delicate ones – that is, all females – from mere contact with anything that could offend. It is a truism that exposure to all manner of things changes the responses. Exposure to unpleasant things can 'harden' a person, but this is not necessarily a misfortune. To take an obvious example, most of us would regard it as both normal and desirable that a trained nurse should remain unflustered in the presence of accident or sudden illness, while a less experienced person might give proof of their delicacy and sensibility by fainting, or doing something else equally unhelpful.

Many women must have been far less 'delicate' than they led others to believe. They could scarcely have survived otherwise, especially once they had become mothers. The changing social patterns in England undoubtedly had a lot to do with the tendency to erect a fence around women, protecting them from the real world, but in due course the notions of propriety which came into vogue affected not just women, but all aspects of social behaviour. When class had been more or less fixed by birth and breeding, the rich could afford to be as plain-speaking as the peasantry without any fear of anyone confusing them with one another. The industrial revolution led to great social (and geographical) mobility; the middle classes grew apace, and their aspirations to move up in the world, aided by the substantial fortunes which were now within their reach, led to new standards of behaviour. The womenfolk had to be seen to be ladies of leisure, and were in

2 Lovers on a bed. A painting from the House of the Centenary in Pompeii. 1st century AD

themselves status symbols, like money and other property. The fidelity and utter dependency of wives was crucial to safeguard the families and the dynasties of the *nouveaux riches*. At the same time the Victorian paterfamilias, struggling during his working hours in the far from gentlemanly rat-race of commerce, had romantic ideas about the innocence and purity of the family circle where he relaxed. John Ruskin expresses the idea in this passage from *Sesame and Lilies* (1868):

This is the true nature of home – it is the place of Peace; the shelter, not only from all injury, but from all terror, doubt, and division. In so far as it is not this, it is not home; so far as the anxieties of the outer life penetrate into it, and the inconsistently minded, unknown, unloved, or hostile society of the outer world is allowed by either husband or wife to cross the threshold, it ceases to be home . . .

None of this applies to the unfortunate lower classes, on whose labour the fortunes of the rich were built; their homes were grimmer than ever, and no doubt their behaviour as gross as ever. The sordid underside of Victorian society was also an integral part of the pattern.

Another aspect of the middle-class ideal in Victorian society was the rapid growth in the reading public. Just as television has taken over and dominated leisure in the latter half of the twentieth century, so reading, often reading aloud in the family circle, was enormously important in the nineteenth. This trend had also been well under way since the last decades of the eighteenth century, with inexpensive novels and circulating libraries totally changing the pattern of book-owning and reading. Books had been the prerogative of the rich and highly educated, but were now widely distributed. The more available a medium is, the blander it has to be. There are more prejudices to offend.

The story of literary expurgation is wittily and instructively told in Noel Perrin's book *Dr Bowdler's Legacy*, and this is not the place to discuss it in detail. The important point to note is that whatever the motives of the expurgators (and those of at least some of them were undoubtedly utterly sincere), the growth of this practice led to dishonest scholarship. Many methods were used to excise the direct or crude ideas and expressions of such bawdy writers as Shakespeare – some of them simply succeeded in drawing attention to the offending matter – but they included the tacit suppression of portions of text, misleading the reader into thinking it complete. Occasionally, where words were sufficiently obsolete, as in Middle English, there are even examples of deliberately false glosses: an 1860 editor of the fifteenth-century Scots poet William Dunbar did not cut out the word *swyfe*, but instead told the surprised reader that it meant 'to sing and play'. No doubt by this time people had become so innocent that many of them believed him, though a truly 'delicate' spirit should surely have sensed and swooned at any synonym, however archaic, for 'copulate'. Though this kind of thing is certainly funny, the attitude which places propriety before truth is not.

Expurgation of literature in English is one thing, but the classics are something else. Though the young could be, and were, protected against the bawdiness of Greek and Latin authors by suitable selection of material for school curricula, once adult a man who had had the right sort of education automatically qualified as a person who could safely read such heady stuff. Fluent knowledge of Greek and Latin, with its implication of high social status, has always conferred this benefit, along with many others. The tendency to put improper passages into

3 A phallus carved as an apotropaic symbol on a wall in a Roman city, Leptis Magna in Libya.

Latin, even where the main body of a work was in the vernacular, ensured that only 'suitable' persons could read the work. Even knowledge of modern foreign languages was enough at times, and there are many translations of Boccaccio's *Decameron* in which the bawdy bits are left in Italian. Another example of the same idea is an important early twentieth-century volume on Gallo-Roman pottery (published in 1904) in which the French text gives way to Latin when decoration of a sexual nature is described. Knowledge of foreign, and especially ancient, languages defined one's position as superior; one was certainly educated, probably rich, and very likely male, all qualities which made it permissible to read material denied to the weaker vessels, the ignorant, poor and female. Nonetheless, Victorian prudery was such that 'impropriety' in the classics was assiduously avoided even by many educated, rich adult males, and its existence was certainly regarded by them as a regrettable lapse of proper feeling on the part of the ancient authors concerned. Classical culture, especially the Greek, which was more highly regarded than Roman, was rather selectively admired.

It is hardly surprising that in this atmosphere the existence of openly sexual motifs in classical artefacts was a fact which was as far as possible suppressed, and that those who suppressed it were able also to set aside the guilt which a scholar should feel about this kind of manipulation of the evidence.

If we return to the history of collecting and archaeology in this period, we will see that one of the most important factors was the rediscovery by accident, early in the eighteenth century, of the sites of Pompeii and Herculaneum. Though the early phases of excavation there were kept fairly secret, by 1757 the first of a series of illustrated volumes on the antiquities of Herculaneum started to appear, revealing a wealth of detail about daily life in the first century AD which must have been a revelation to all. The impetus to collecting and study was very great. The volume which contained descriptions and illustrations of the sexually explicit

4 Leda and the Swan: a Roman wall-
painting from Herculaneum.
1st century AD

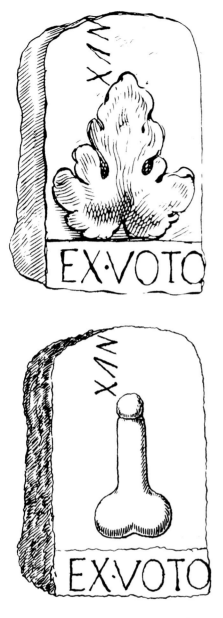

5 A votive phallic carving on a stone from Roman Scotland, (*top*) as figured by John Horsley in his *Britannia Romana* (1732), and (*above*) in the 1865 edition of Richard Payne Knight's *Discourse on the Worship of Priapus*.

material was a separate one, and it, in particular, must have been astonishing to many readers. The apparent casualness with which first-century Romans surrounded themselves with images of the phallus must have been a surprise even to the mid-eighteenth century, not yet as sensitive to such matters as their Victorian descendents. After all, an unmistakable representation of the male organ is a lot more direct than even the ripest language, and is understandable to all. Even in 1732 John Horsley, in his splendid book on Roman Britain, *Britannia Romana*, had jibbed at illustrating a stone with such a figure on it and had substituted a vine-leaf (5); his text also contains a very perceptible seed of the delicacy which later grew to such overwhelming proportions:

At *Westerwood* fort was found a remarkable *Priapus* or *fallus*, now also in the same Baron's collection. Below it is EX VOTO, and at the top these letters XAN, which I read *decem annorum*; and may denote perhaps the continuance of some indisposition, upon the recovery from which this was erected; or else the time of barrenness, after which a child was obtained. But decency forbids the saying any more on this subject, as it obliges me to conceal the figure.

The decency seems a little half-hearted, in that he has already told us that the carving was of a 'fallus'; scholarship has not been totally neglected. A century later, we would at the most be told that the inscription was 'gross' or 'improper': more likely the offending stone would not have been mentioned at all. The engraving of the same stone in the 1865 reprint of Richard Payne Knight's *Discourse on the Worship of Priapus* is a special case, and we shall look in greater detail at this publication below (10). It is interesting that the presence of vine-leaves, like asterisks in an expurgated text, tend to inflame the imagination, sometimes leading to thoughts of greater impropriety than is actually there. In another early eighteenth-century example, a small Gallo-Roman Venus figurine, engraved wearing a tiny acanthus leaf, looks decidedly more provocative than in its normal state of nudity.

The true scholars of the second half of the eighteenth century were able to face the facts of Greek and Roman impropriety. Some of them, like Payne Knight, were sufficiently intrigued to make a special study of the matter, though without thereby neglecting other aspects of ancient civilisation. Nor did artists and designers, inspired in a general sense by the discoveries at Pompeii and Herculaneum, wholly ignore the material contained in the volume devoted to erotica. There is a terracotta version by the distinguished sculptor Joseph Nollekens (1737–1823) of the notorious Herculaneum marble of Pan copulating with a goat (7, 1).

An anecdote about the sculptor well illustrates the harshness of advancing purity at this period. In the early sixteenth century in Italy a set of twenty engravings taken from drawings by Giulio Romano were published. They depicted different aspects and positions of sexual intercourse, and the poet Pietro Aretino wrote sonnets on the same theme to accompany sixteen of them. The engravings, popularly known as *I Modi*, circulated for generations, and it is said that Nollekens acquired in Rome one of the last sets extant, perhaps the very last. His confessor came upon him one day when he was looking at them and to Nollekens' eternal regret, forced him to destroy them. Art cannot soften the heart of prudery.

On the whole, it is true to say that members of the group of scholars and collectors who were at work in England towards the end of the eighteenth century were capable of studying the ever-increasing body of classical antiquities in a sane, balanced and open manner. They belonged to the old order of the aristocratic and educated; they were not frightened of being corrupted themselves, and they were probably not as yet fully aware of the tide of prudery which was beginning to rise around them. They were members of the Society of Dilettanti, Fellows of the still young Society of Antiquaries of London, and many were major benefactors of the British Museum, which had come into being, itself based on magnificent private collections, in the 1750s. They were more concerned, as any scholar should be, with the advance of knowledge than with contemporary sensibilities.

It is worth looking in detail at some of these collectors and scholars, in particular those who collected and published objects which were later found offensive to Victorian taste. One who is interesting for a special reason, though he stands a little apart from the group, is the so-called Chevalier d'Hancarville, a French scholar and adventurer whose real name was Pierre-François Hugues. He was born in Nancy in 1729, and travelled very widely, becoming friendly with many classical scholars of note. One of these was Sir William Hamilton (the husband of Nelson's Lady Hamilton), who made good use of his position as Envoy Extraordinary to the Court of Naples, to which he was appointed in 1764, for collecting some of the choice antiquities which were available in that area at the time. D'Hancarville catalogued and illustrated part of Hamilton's collection in four fine volumes which were published in Naples in 1766–7. In addition, however, he went well beyond the bounds of scholarship, and indulged in some flights of fancy of his own. His works on the private lives of the Caesars and the secret cults of Roman women were illustrated with engravings allegedly based on ancient engraved gems and coins, but actually in great measure his own inventions. Described with appropriate quotations from ancient authors, they display a hearty, and sometimes witty, taste for the obscene. To go further in this direction than the Greeks and Romans did themselves was unusual at the time, and was of course very misleading to others. The important fact is that d'Hancarville, who in spite of this regrettable lapse into what can only be called faking was a genuinely learned man, was a friend of such scholars as Payne Knight, Hamilton and Townley, and was not thought ill of by them for his interest in ancient erotica.

Much of the material in Hamilton's collections found its way in due course to the British Museum, as did the outstanding collection of Richard Payne Knight. Payne Knight, who was born about 1750, was a man of real distinction, a gentleman, who inherited extensive estates and looked after them assiduously, but who also found time to study ancient languages and literature, to collect classical bronzes and other antiquities, to write extensively on a very wide range of subjects (including some poetry which is said to be better forgotten), to be a Member of Parliament (a Whig), and to set himself up, with good reason, as a general arbiter of taste. His very first published work was the one which brought down on his head the wrath of those who in 1786, when it appeared, were further advanced in the coming trend of prudery than Knight himself. It was entitled, in the comprehensive manner of the time: *An Account of the Remains of the Worship of Priapus, lately existing at Isernia, in the Kingdom of Naples: In Two Letters; One from Sir William Hamilton, K.B. His Majesty's Minister at the Court of Naples, to Sir Joseph Banks, Bart., President of the Royal Society; The other from a person residing at Isernia.*

6 An engraving in an eighteenth-century French publication (B. de Montfaucon, *L'Antiquité expliquée*, vol.v(ii), pl.cxxxvi, Paris, 1722), of a standard type of small terracotta figurine of Venus, made in Gaul in the second century AD. The acanthus leaf is an eighteenth-century addition.

7 Pan and a goat. A small terracotta sculpture by Joseph Nollekens (1737–1823), based on the famous ancient marble statuette from Herculaneum.

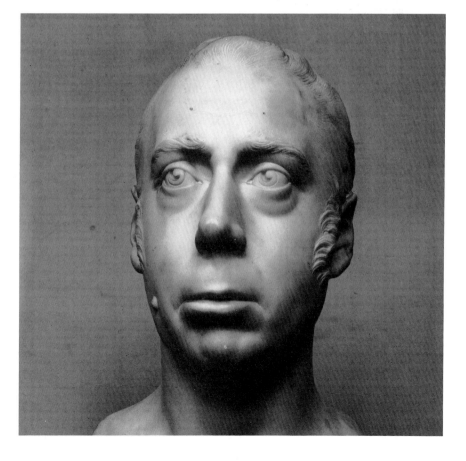

8 A marble portrait bust of Richard Payne Knight (1750–1824). Knight was one of the foremost collectors and antiquarians of his time, and a major benefactor of the British Museum.

9 Red-figure vase by the Dinos Painter,
with a homosexual scene: from the
collection of Sir William Hamilton.
450–425 BC

*To which is added, A DISCOURSE ON THE WORSHIP OF PRIAPUS, and its
Connection with the mystic Theology of the Ancients. With 18 Plates. By R.P.Knight,
Esq. London.*

The letter from Hamilton which is the starting-point of this publication is an
extremely interesting and significant account of the survival of the use of phallic
votives in a small town near Naples in the 1780s. The purchase and donation of
phalluses made of wax took place within a Christian context, as gifts to Saints
Cosimo and Damian, but the practice must have been part of an unbroken
tradition stretching back to Roman times. Isernia itself, incidentally, was
destroyed in one of the earthquakes to which the Naples area is so tragically
liable, on 26 July 1805. Hamilton arranged for specimens of the fragile wax
votives to be sent to the British Museum. The other letter, in Italian, adds nothing
to Hamilton's account, but is presumably the source of it.

Payne Knight's own *Discourse* is naturally the *raison d'être* of the book, and it is
a wide-ranging discussion of pagan beliefs and practices which is by no means
concerned only with the subject of the title. The style is standard eighteenth-
century-erudite, the language entirely proper, some of the ideas more than a little
far-fetched, and the whole thing very far from being licentious or sexually
stimulating. It aroused censure at the time, so much so that Payne Knight tried to
withdraw copies from circulation, and it certainly marked its author, in the view
of later commentators, as completely beyond the pale. A judgement frequently
quoted is that of a person called Thomas Mathias, the editor of a literary journal

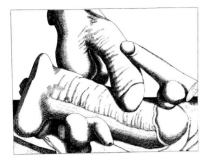

10 Engraving, from Richard Payne Knight's *Discourse on the Worship of Priapus*, of wax phallic votives still in use at Isernia, near Naples, in the late eighteenth century.

11 Actual examples of the eighteenth-century wax phallic votives from Isernia.

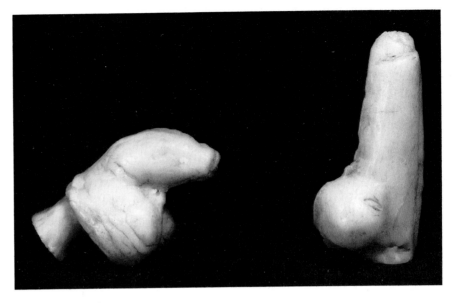

entitled *The Pursuits of Literature*, and an early advocate and practitioner of the craft of expurgation. Of poor Payne Knight's essay, he wrote in 1808: 'One of the most unbecoming and indecent treatises which ever disgraced the pen of a man who would be considered a scholar and a philosopher'. One cannot help wondering whether Mathias actually read it, or whether the title page and the plates were enough for him. Later, an officer of the very institution which had most benefited by Payne Knight's collecting activities, the British Museum, was able to write in terms even more severe. Edward Hawkins, Keeper of the Department of Antiquities from 1826 to 1860, compiled a manuscript catalogue of bronzes which included brief biographies of the donors of important collections. His venomous comments on Richard Payne Knight are of great interest in illustrating the almost hysterical fear of any subject connected with sex, and any discussion of religion other than protestant Christianity, which was so characteristic of the nineteenth century.

Hawkins says of the *Discourse on the Worship of Priapus*: 'Of this work it is impossible to speak in terms of reprobation sufficiently strong; it is a work too gross almost to mention; and it is quite impossible to quote the indignant but too descriptive language of the critics in their severe but just remarks upon this disgusting production . . .' In other words, even the hostile reviews of the eighteenth century on this subject were too much for the delicate nineteenth-century constitution to stand. Hawkins goes on to list Payne Knight's publications on other subjects, gleefully noting adverse contemporary criticism wherever possible, till he comes to *An Inquiry into the Symbolical Language of Ancient Art and Mythology*, which was separately printed in 1818 and appeared again in 1835 (after the author's death), as had always been intended, as an appendix to the second volume of *Specimens of Ancient Sculpture*, published by the Society of Dilettanti. Payne Knight offends Hawkins here in his religious attitude: 'With every thing connected with the operations of the Holy Spirit and with the mediation and atonement of the Redeemer there is not any trace of his having the least acquaintance'. This is most unlikely to be true, for Payne Knight was an educated man; it was simply that he did not wish to interpret antiquity in terms of

Christian theology. Notice that the Victorian refinement in speech and writing extended to religious as well as sexual matters, and the name of Christ, even when correctly and respectfully used, was too strong to endure.

In summary, Hawkins says of this work:

We lament, deeply lament, that the 'Inquiry into the symbolical language of Ancient Art and Mythology' was ever printed at all, and still more so that it has been inserted in that splendid volume of 'Select Specimens of Ancient Art', which it has made a sealed volume, unsafe and unfit to be subjected to the perusal of any young people of either sex. To a young man of classical taste, and a fondness and feeling for works of ancient art, we know not of any volume so dangerous as the 'Inquiry'. It has a direct tendency to undermine the principles by polluting the imagination, and investing all classical literature, and every object of ancient art with irremovable impurity. It is not to a grossness of language that may disgust, or to a vivid description which may excite, that we are now objecting, but to the entire principle of interpretation which pervades the whole book. This work is the most complete specimen of Monomania, which was ever exhibited to the world; in every object of nature or of art, the writer perceives nothing but symbols and personifications of the one gross idea, which has taken entire and absolute possession of his mind, and has created an atmosphere of grossness and impurity which is dangerous to approach.

To do him justice, Hawkins also quotes a memoir of Payne Knight which appeared after his death in 1824. This comments, amongst other things: 'He was admired by his neighbours for his exemplary conduct, beloved by his tenants for his kindness and indulgence to them, and sanctified by the prayers and blessings of the poor, to whom he was a most liberal benefactor'. It must have struck Hawkins and other Victorian puritans that these Christian virtues were surprising qualities to find in so depraved a scholar.

Payne Knight was what we should now call a man of liberal tastes and beliefs, who had the misfortune to publish his researches at a time when the tide of manners was turning. Different judgements of his work appeared, naturally enough, in the publications of those who pursued similar interests, even in the very teeth of Victorianism, but by the late nineteenth century even more general writers saw him in a more balanced way. Edward Edwards, author of *Lives of the Founders of the British Museum*, published in 1870, has this to say about the *Inquiry into the Symbolical Language . . .*, which so incensed Hawkins:

The student will gain from the Inquiry real knowledge about ancient art. He will find, indeed, not a few statements which the author himself would be the first to modify in the light of the new information of the last fifty years. But he will also find much which, in its time, proved to be suggestive and fruitful to other minds, and which prepared the way for wider and deeper studies. It may do so yet. The book is one which the student of archaeology cannot afford to overlook.

Even on the notorious *Discourse*, Edwards's comments are a shake of the head rather than a scream of rage: '. . . a subject which scarcely any one will now think to have been well chosen, as the firstfruits or earnest of a scholarly career'. The hysteria was dying down.

The *Discourse* was reprinted several times, and the reprint of 1865 is one of special importance. It is noteworthy that at this date the publisher who was found willing to bring it out, John Camden Hotten, was also a publisher of outright pornography. In 1865 even serious work on such a subject could appear only as part of that sub-culture, not as a respectable piece of scholarship. This edition reprints Payne Knight's text and plates, and appends to it *An Essay on the Worship*

12 *above* A small Roman bronze statuette of Hermaphrodite, a piece from the collection of Richard Payne Knight. 1st–2nd century AD

13 *opposite* An example of a Greek vase from the collection of George Witt: a black-figure vessel by the Acheloos Painter depicting a satyr and maenad. Late 6th century BC

of the Generative Powers during the Middle Ages of Western Europe. This essay, more readable and a good deal more plain-spoken than Payne Knight's – the authors, after all, knew that they were appearing in the high-class pornography market, whereas Payne Knight had no such thought – was written by 'one of the most distinguished English antiquaries . . . assisted, it is understood, by two prominent Fellows of the Royal Society'. According to Henry Spencer Ashbee, the Victorian bibliographer and yet another munificent benefactor of the British Museum, these were Mr Thomas Wright, Sir James Emerson Tennent, and Mr George Witt.

The last named of these is a character of some interest, and the story of his collection and its donation to the British Museum illustrates many points about the ever more severe attitude to 'indecent' antiquities in the nineteenth century. Payne Knight and his contemporaries did not collect only phallic objects or those with some sexual connotation; it was simply that they did not avoid them. Payne Knight was keenly interested in them, as any honest person might be, for the information they gave about the different attitudes to these matters in antiquity. Witt specialised far more. Apart from an early natural history collection, his main interests were antiquities relating to the Roman baths and objects which were, by nineteenth-century standards, obscene.

George Witt has a far lower profile as a 'founder of the British Museum' than Payne Knight; indeed, he is a positively elusive character, and very little has been published about him. He was born in Norfolk in about 1803 or 1804, and entered Leyden University in Holland to study medicine in 1828. One presumes he must have had some previous study of the subject behind him, for he graduated MD in 1830 with a thesis on cholera which was subsequently published. On returning to England as a qualified doctor, he took up an appointment at the Bedford County Infirmary, eventually becoming Physician to that institution. In the year 1834 he was elected a Fellow of the Royal Society, and was also Mayor of Bedford. His obituary in the *Bedfordshire Mercury* many years later reflects the success of this phase of his career: 'Doctor Witt was at one time as familiar to our town and county as a household word'. But in the late 1840s he emigrated to Australia, and after some years practising medicine in Sydney he appears to have given up his profession, dropping even the title 'Doctor' from his name. Instead, he became a banker, and proved as successful in this as in his first career. When he returned to England around 1854 he was a rich man, able to indulge his taste for collecting antiquities. He took up residence in London, and it is said that he used to hold Sunday morning lectures, presumably for a very carefully selected audience, on his collection of phallic antiquities. An illness in 1865 made him consider the fate of this collection, which he rightly considered to be one of great importance. In November of that year, he wrote to Anthony Panizzi, the Director of the British Museum, in the following terms:

Dear Sir,
During my late severe illness it was a source of much regret to me that I had not made such a disposition of my Collection of 'Symbols of the Early Worship of Mankind', as, combined with its due preservation, would have enabled me in some measure to have superintended its arrangement.

In accordance with this feeling I now propose to present my Collection to the British Museum, with the hope that some small room may be appointed for its reception in which may also be deposited and arranged the important specimens, already in the vaults of the Museum – and elsewhere, which are illustrative of the same subject.

The Trustees of the Museum, perhaps somewhat surprisingly (but Museum Trustees are often charmingly unpredictable) accepted the gift, and the Witt Collection duly came to the Museum. There were other donations from Witt over the next couple of years, chiefly connected with his other great interest, the Roman baths. It is significant that Witt himself envisaged his collection as part of a larger group of objects 'illustrative of the same subject' and, indeed, this is exactly how the material was treated in the Museum. Well before the time of Witt's gift in 1865 it had been decided to separate out the 'indecent' material, formerly mixed in with everything else, and form it into a *Museum Secretum*, perhaps along the lines of the 'secret' collection of the Naples Museum. Thus, the objects which had come in, for example, with Payne Knight's collection, were

14 A bronze vessel-handle with an erotic scene, from Pompeii, a piece from the *museum secretum* of the Naples Museum. 1st century AD

already set aside solely on account of their obscenity in the eyes of the nineteenth century: this was held to be their leading characteristic. The same approach was applied to the classification of books, giving rise to the Private Case of the British Museum Library, now the British Library. Witt himself died in February 1869, his place in the Museum's history assured. The *Museum Secretum*, or rather its remnants, tended until very recently to be familiarly, though inaccurately, referred to as the 'Witt Collection'.

We will consider the later history of the *Museum Secretum* in a moment. First, it is worth considering in more detail the implications of this type of collection. The function of archaeology is to infer from the material remains some information about the people and the society which created them. However much one may enjoy and admire an object for its own sake, in itself a perfectly proper and valid response, the purposes of archaeology are not served until one goes beyond this point. Private collectors may collect for many reasons: for aesthetic pleasure alone; for mercenary motives – art as investment, the most reprehensible reason for collecting; or they may, as many of them did, and still do, have a serious academic interest in the material as well. Anyone claiming to be an archaeologist must have the latter impulse. Consequently, any object has an interest and potential importance, beyond its beauty or strangeness to modern eyes, for the information it may convey. The archaeologist can gain access to this information by identifying for each single object a whole range of features, including the type of object within a system of classification, its provenance (meaning, in archaeology, the place where it was found), its context (its archaeological relationship with other finds), its date, naturally, and its technology. The way in which objects are arranged and categorised in museums is consequently a very complex question and will depend on factors such as the overall size and scope of the collection and its general aims. A museum primarily concerned with the history of art and technology will classify things somewhat differently from one which is based on cultural, more archaeological, divisions. In the first, all bronze statuettes will go together, whether they are Roman, African, Oriental or modern; in the latter, all Roman objects, whether they are of metal, fired clay or organic materials, will form a broad category. The *leading* characteristic of an object will therefore be interpreted differently according to the general system in use. There will inevitably be difficult cases and some contradictions, since antiquities are not simple things.

The concept of the *Museum Secretum* runs counter to the arrangement described above for either a culturally based museum or an art-based one or, indeed, for almost any other kind one can imagine. What happened in the early part of the nineteenth century was that obscenity to modern eyes – not even obscenity in the view of the creators of the objects – started to be seen as a characteristic which overrode all others. Thus, in the British Museum, antiquities which in terms of sexual decency offended the somewhat specialised sensibilities of the nineteenth-century observer were all put together, whether they were classical, medieval or modern, made of clay, metal or wax, from Europe or the Orient, and so on. All were housed, for no particular reason that we can now detect except the historical one that they stayed where they were when the first subdivision of antiquities departments occurred in 1861, in the Department of British and Mediaeval Antiquities. 'Obscenity' is not a scholarly category, it is a moral one, and it is academically indefensible. But this approach seemed so self-

15 Applied decorative medallions from pottery vessels made in the Rhône valley in the Roman period. As well as erotic themes, scenes from the circus and amphitheatre were very popular on this type of pottery. 2nd–3rd century AD

evident in the middle of the nineteenth century that even a collector like George Witt, who certainly had a genuine academic interest in his material, fully expected his artefacts to be put aside with others of a like nature. He would not have expected the Roman bronzes to go with other Roman bronzes, the black-figure vases with other black-figure vases. These things were obscene first and foremost. That was the basis on which he had collected them.

This setting aside of material has many adverse effects. The objects are more difficult of access, and can easily be overlooked when compiling catalogues according to more enlightened classifications, even if they are not deliberately held back. Individual objects which may be rare or important in some way quite unconnected with their sexual decoration or form may also fail to be taken into account in more general work. Furthermore, they acquire one of the irritating characteristics shared by material made of precious metals: they become more valuable in purely monetary terms than similar pieces with non-erotic decoration. Objects made of gold or silver do have to have special treatment in museum terms because of their intrinsic value, but at least this is still a true reflection of their status in antiquity. If we keep gold Roman rings apart from bronze and iron ones, we do no more than reflect their greater value in their own time. But there is no evidence to suggest that a samian bowl with erotic decoration was more valuable than one ornamented with a hunting scene, and it is absurd to part it from its fellows in a modern museum.

The *Museum Secretum* started quietly to break down even before the First World War, and by now most of the objects are at least in the Departments to which they should belong. This is not a simple matter in itself, since departmental categories have shifted shape like witches in a fairy-tale since the 1860s, when the British Museum's general Department of Antiquities started to subdivide. When the Morel Collection of French antiquities of prehistoric, Roman and medieval date

16 Mould for an Arretine vase from the workshop of Marcus Perennius at Arezzo. The figures of lovers on Arretine ware by this manufacturer are by far the finest on any type of Roman ceramic, and their influence is clearly to be seen on later decoration of the same type. Late 1st century BC

came to the Museum in 1901, the British and Mediaeval Department initially retained the 'indecent' Gallo-Roman objects like the Rhône valley pottery medallions (15) for the *Museum Secretum*, while passing all other Roman antiquities to the Greek and Roman Department. But within a very few years they found their way to their proper home. Scholarship was beginning to rebel against delicacy.

Quite apart from creating this artificial and unworkable category of antiquities, Victorian prudery built an edifice of academically unsound conclusions on the existence of ancient erotica. A fine example of the curious reasoning which was brought to bear on this subject is to be found in a French work, published as late as 1934, but in the true nineteenth-century spirit. It is a major study of the samian pottery made at the South Gaulish site of La Graufesenque, near Millau (Tarn). The author, the Abbé Frédéric Hermet, was too sound a scholar to exclude the erotic subjects which often occur on this ware, but he grouped the illustrations together on one plate, and he had this to say about them (I translate):

As long as Roman civilisation was not thoroughly established in Gaul, during the reigns of Tiberius, Claudius and Nero, the potters did not figure any erotic subjects on their ware, endeavouring not to shock or alienate their clientele. It was only when Gaul was completely romanised, under Vespasian and above all under Domitian and Trajan, that such scenes appear on sigillata vases. This fact is a palpable proof that the Romans imported into Gaul, along with civilisation, the corruption of morals.

3 Red-figure wine-cooler (*psykter*) by Douris, with revelling satyrs. The balancing feat performed by the central satyr is nullified by the expurgation shown in 2, and the humour is lost. *c.*500–470 BC

There are several arguable statements in this, not least the suggestion that Gaul, which became a Roman province in the first century BC, was not completely romanised until the late first AD, or even the early second century (the reign of Trajan), and the implication that the pre-Roman Iron Age Gauls were not civilised. It all depends, no doubt, on what one means by civilisation. But far more important than this, Hermet can sustain his argument only by ignoring a fact which must surely have been well known and obvious to him as a great samian scholar: the rarity of erotic figure-types until the reign of Vespasian is due primarily to the relative rarity of all human figures in samian decoration up to that time. (A figure-type is a decorative motif of a person or animal, as opposed to one showing an inanimate object.) Until the late first century AD, the most popular shape of bowl in this mass-produced ware had very narrow zones of decoration. After this, the new popular shape has a larger area for relief ornament, like the earlier Italian Arretine ware, and a range of human figure-types, including some erotic ones, becomes normal. This is exactly the kind of stylistic point which Hermet studies in great detail in the rest of his book, but when dealing with the 'obscene' he chooses to ignore it and use the evidence to support quite different conclusions.

Furthermore, Hermet is displaying a confusion between doing and depicting which is still a common problem of purity campaigners. He can hardly have supposed that the ancient Gauls were ignorant of sexual intercourse until introduced to this decadent practice by the conquering Romans: the objection

4 *left* An erotic scene in low relief on a bronze bowl from Pompeii. The male figure is a satyr (he has animal ears and a small tail), the female either a nymph or maenad. 1st century BC – 1st century AD

17 Sherd from a samian bowl made in South Gaul, with a figure-type of an ithyphallic flute-playing satyr. The relative rarity of such figures on the earlier products of this important Gallo-Roman industry is due to the fact that human figures were seldom used on the earlier shapes of bowl: the inference that Roman influence gradually depraved the naturally innocent native Gauls is a false one. Late 1st to early 2nd century AD

18, 19 Two Italian volute lamps of the first century AD, one decorated with a gladiatorial scene, the other with a pair of lovers.

must be that morals will be undermined by the visual representation of such an activity on a common utensil. If one objects totally to the very existence of sex, then certainly a picture of it must be offensive, but if one accepts that it is not a bad thing *per se*, no-one has ever satisfactorily demonstrated why it should be wrong to depict or describe it. Pictures of undoubtedly bad behaviour (for example, killing people) are rarely objected to even on the basis that the activities they depict are actually morally wrong. The two illustrations (18) and (19) show two Roman lamps made in Italy in the first century AD, archaeologically in the same category and of equal interest. One has a scene taken from the Roman amphitheatre, where gladiators fought to the death in the name of entertainment and the sand was stained with blood. One would imagine that most of us would disapprove of the activity shown, but it does not prevent us from studying the object for what it can tell us about this least-acceptable of Roman customs, nor should it prevent us. The other lamp shows a pair of lovers on a bed, a somewhat more universal theme. Is it too much to expect that we should be able to display the same degree of objectivity towards this?

The Victorian belief that sexual customs which were different from their own were not only morally wrong, but were the cause of most of the ills that befell the society in which they were practised, was taken to great extremes. There is no doubt that for many, there was an equation which went: 'sexual immorality equals general degeneracy, equals social and economic collapse'. Even now there is a popular belief that the 'fall of the Roman Empire' was attributable to a great degree to sexual excess, and a popular belief of this kind is a vestige of an earlier academic attitude. It should hardly be necessary to say that no single fact can explain the rise or the fall of an empire; the process is infinitely complex and involves almost every strand in the fabric of society. In any case, there is no good reason to suppose that the Romans indulged in sexual excess compared with other peoples of antiquity or with ourselves. They were merely less reticent than some in talking about and depicting sexual matters. It is true that they were inclined to say things which damaged their own case. They accused the Etruscans of 'luxury', and attributed the dissolution and absorption of their culture in that of Rome to this cause; Tacitus, writing in the first century AD, speaks highly of the barbarian Germans, contrasting them with the soft and luxury-loving Romans of his own day. The qualities being pinpointed as destructive in these pep-talks were general high-living rather than specifically sexual looseness, but such writings, and those of the more colourful satirists, provided useful ammunition for Victorian commentators.

The selectiveness of the Victorians in this matter is interesting. While criticising the Roman Empire freely, their attitude towards Greek culture was very different. The admiration for the ancient Greeks in nineteenth-century England was intense, and the evidence in both literature and art that the Greeks and the Romans had very much the same attitude towards sexual matters, and the same cheerful abandon in depicting them, seems to have been tacitly ignored for much of the time. The cruelty of the Romans, as opposed to the Greeks, was also blatantly overstated, and still is. The public entertainments of the arena which I have just mentioned were undoubtedly vile, but cruelty and violence were endemic in ancient times. The Greeks, Celts, Romans and all peoples of antiquity regarded violence and slavery as part of everyday life, not to mention the ferocity of war in this period.

In any case, the Victorian English were in a poor position to criticise this particular aspect of antiquity. They had no moral scruples about waging war, and most were content to see the poor live in conditions which would certainly not have seemed luxurious to the poorest slaves of ancient Rome. In the sexual area, they had enthusiastically taken to a particularly violent form of gratification, flagellation and even worse forms of sado-masochism being very common at this period. Another aspect of this hypocrisy was the flourishing trade in child prostitution. Yet these Victorians were the people who were too refined to look at a Roman bronze phallus without blushing.

The separate treatment which erotic antiquities have received has been damaging to scholarship, and even now, when the trend at last is moving in the opposite direction, the effects are far from forgotten. No-one has yet, to my knowledge, clearly stated the distinction between consciously erotic ancient art and representations which may seem erotic to our eyes, but to their creators were religious or apotropaic. Naturally, many scholars are well aware of this, but it is not popularly understood. Yet one would have thought that this, in itself, was an interesting facet of the ancient attitude to sex. Expurgated texts cast long shadows in that they often continue to be available and to confuse and mislead readers long after correct versions have become acceptable again. In the same way, the treatment of antiquities which are thought to be indecent as a category apart from all others has a long-term effect. Their absence can affect the conclusions of scholarly studies which are otherwise standard works, and the normal proportion of such objects among other artefacts in antiquity is impossible to assess. Our already biased and unbalanced sources of information are wilfully biased even further. In this aspect of study, we have two hundred years of distorted scholarship to catch up on and to correct.

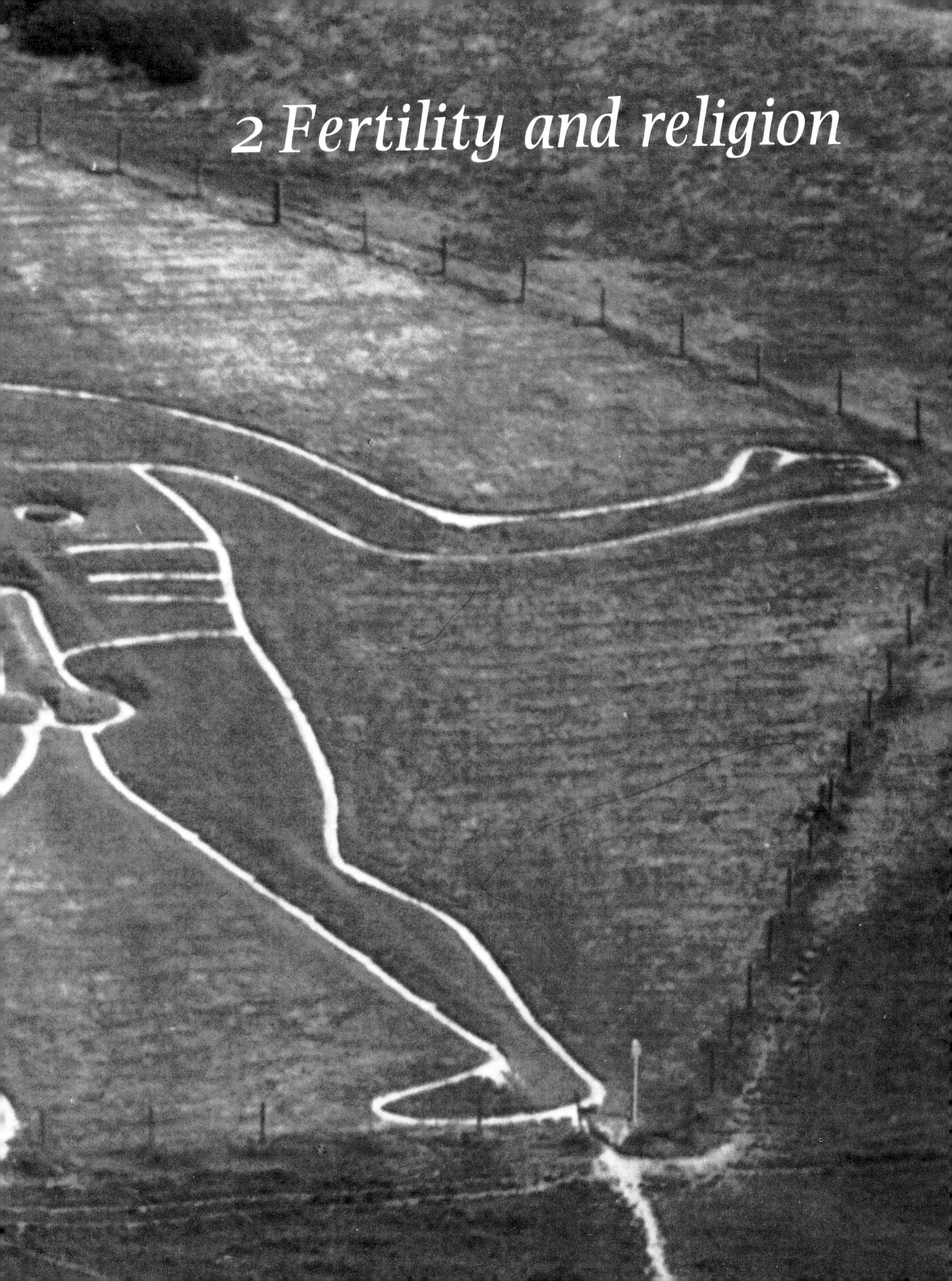

2 Fertility and religion

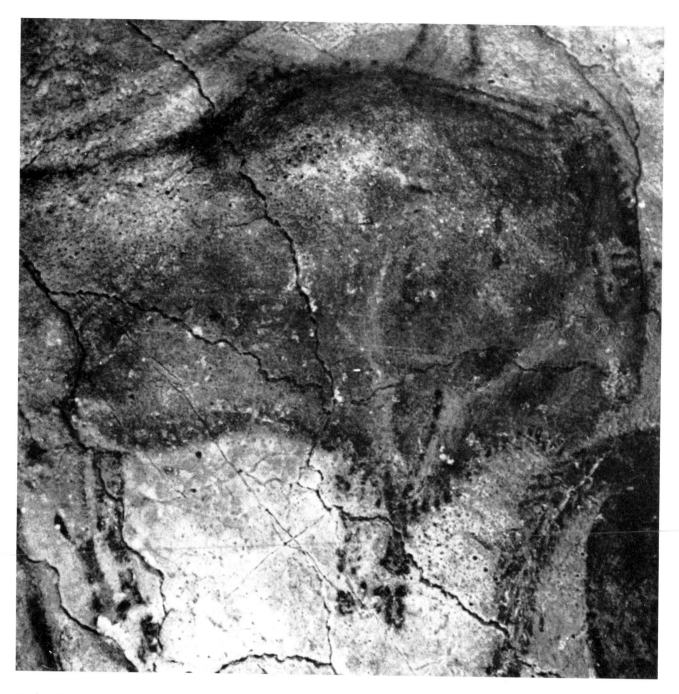

21 *above* Stone-age cave-painting of a
bison from Altamira in Spain.

20 *previous page* The giant of Cerne
Abbas, Dorset, a phallic hill-figure perhaps
representing Hercules, and possibly of
Romano-British origin.

It is well known that fertility was a major preoccupation of most early religions, and it is all too easy for a modern city-dweller to find this fact amusing or faintly embarrassing. People who live in towns have never given much thought to the source of the food they buy and the difficulties which might have had to be overcome in its production, so the idea of fertility as a subject of earnest prayer and strenuous ritual may seem strange and alien to them. The farmer, even the farmer surrounded by the sophisticated machinery of the twentieth century, will find the idea a lot easier to grasp: unseasonable weather, disease and pests are still a source of real anxiety, and though a failed crop may nowadays, in an advanced country, merely spell reduced profits rather than starvation, there are still cases where adverse natural forces can cause the ruin of a family which makes its living from keeping stock or growing crops. The peasant, at any place or period, has no difficulty in believing that fertility, both animal and vegetable, is the key not merely to comfort, but to actual survival. If life is to go on, the seed which has been sown must germinate and eventually result in a good harvest, and the animals, if they are to go on producing meat, milk and wool, must not only be healthy, but must breed. The modern observer is too easily side-tracked by the thought that the processes of vegetable growth and animal reproduction are full of fascination and wonder, even to those who study them in a purely scientific spirit, and that this is an important factor in the obsession with fertility which characterises so much early religious practice. While this is quite true in itself, far more basic is the fact that if this growth and reproduction does not proceed in the expected fashion, people will starve. The basis of fertility as a religious theme is not mystical, but practical.

Rituals designed to ensure fertility or to celebrate successful breeding or harvest are universal and still widely practised. Even before man had learnt to domesticate animals or tend crops the theme was present. Palaeolithic (Old Stone Age) man lived by hunting and gathering food, and the desire that he should succeed in his hunting, and that the hunted animals should themselves prosper and multiply, was expressed by means of sympathetic magic in the form of paintings and carvings depicting the desired events taking place. Thus mankind's earliest artistic achievements are of a high order, include along with representations of dead and dying animals, animals with young.

The theme of fertility is perhaps most simply and clearly expressed in the form of the mother, and Palaeolithic art includes figurines of pregnant women, presumably to encourage the continuance of the human community. Deities who symbolise and represent motherhood and who protect women in the dangers which this function involves are virtually universal, and remain important in most societies even when other fertility symbols have arisen. The development of agriculture, which led to mankind's first great social revolution, introduced another aspect of fertility, the patient process of sowing seed and tending its growth, and the controlled breeding of domestic animals, in which the male role in reproduction became much clearer than it would have been when men simply hunted herds of wild horses and buffalo for their meat.

The understanding of the male role in reproduction is not instinctive: in the larger animals there is a considerable time lapse between impregnation and even the first recognisable signs of pregnancy, let alone actual birth. Cattle have a period of gestation similar to that of humans, horses even longer (eleven months), while even small animals such as sheep need five and a half months to produce

22 Bronze statuette of Priapus with a robe full of fruit. Fertility is symbolised both by the god's accentuated phallus and by the fruit. 1st–2nd century AD

23 A figure-type found on Gaulish samian pottery of the second century AD, in which the woman appears to be seated on an altar.

their young. Though dogs were probably the first animals to be truly domesticated, their breeding was probably not so closely noted as that of the other species mentioned; even they have a gestation period of over two months, long enough to make the connection between mating and birth far from obvious. The domestication of animals must lead, however, to the recognition of the male contribution to reproduction, and with this new ideas arise, not only about fertility itself, but about property and other social concepts: the mother is no longer seen as the only one responsible for the increase of the population. Our concern with this here is that at this point male fertility deities are introduced, supplementing, though rarely supplanting, the mother-goddess. This whole area of religious practice and development is enormously complex; it is introduced here only as a background to the fairly general discussion below of a few of the fertility deities of classical times.

The period of classical antiquity with which we are dealing covers a time-span of about a thousand years, so it is hardly surprising that there is a great variety of religious ritual, and much which is now very obscure. Obviously there would have been many ancient local fertility festivals connected with events in the agricultural year, and there would have been ancient deities, again often local, who had to be propitiated if the crops and herds were to prosper. In addition, there was the formal Graeco-Roman pantheon, with myths which are often connected with the theme of fertility. Finally, especially in the later period of the Roman Empire, more personal mystery religions from the East, including Christianity, played their part. Since literary evidence, like archaeological evidence, is patchy and incomplete, it would be foolish to imagine that we could make any complete summary of the range and development of this theme in antiquity. All we can do is to consider some of the images which appear to illustrate this religious aspect, rather than straightforward sexual themes, and try to link them with an appropriate deity or ritual.

The range of visual themes which may represent fertility is wide. As we have already noted, there is the mother, pregnant or nursing, or simply a woman with a child. Vegetable fertility is depicted in art by a range of products, particularly grain and fruit. In classical times the cornucopia, or horn of plenty, was a well-established symbol of fruitfulness, and it has also been maintained that the horn is itself a phallic symbol, though it seems doubtful whether this idea was often present in the mind of the artist. The male side of fertility is most easily represented by depicting a male in a state of sexual arousal – an ithyphallic figure – or simply by an image of the phallus alone, a theme to which we shall return in greater detail later. Any or all of these could be involved in religious representations concerning fertility. Finally, fertility can also be implied by scenes depicting mating, whether human or animal, while the actual rites which took place at fertility festivals could also on occasion include overt sexual activity. An illustration of copulation, therefore, may be religious in intention, rather than intended purely for the enjoyment or stimulation of the spectator.

The most basic fertility image, that of the mother, remained popular in classical art. It is, however, somewhat peripheral to our main subject: even the most prudish in recent times have made no objection to statues and statuettes which depict a mother and baby. On the contrary, they have been seen as evidence of tenderness and sensibility on the part of the society and the artists responsible for creating them, a reaction totally unlike that evoked by any graphic representation of sexual activity. It is important to understand that the underlying religious impetus is the same in both cases, and that our diverse reactions are shallow and sentimental. If we accept the genuine and deep importance of fertility gods and rites, then we should be prepared to accept them in whatever guise they appear, not only those which appeal to our own conditioning.

While there are certainly some mother-and-child scenes in both Greek and Roman art which are purely domestic, and are not connected with religion, there is evidence too of mother deities and, probably even more commonly, goddesses who had a special protective role towards women in childbirth and other gynaecological matters. There is no single classical mother-goddess. Demeter (Ceres in Roman mythology) is an earth-mother figure who was primarily concerned with vegetable fertility and the annual cycle of sowing, growth and harvest. She was especially associated with grain. More specifically responsible for childbirth was Artemis (Diana), the hunter-goddess and sister of Apollo; in both Greek and Roman myth she was herself a virgin, and took determined steps to preserve this condition. The Artemis or Diana of the Ephesians who is mentioned in the New Testament was a separate deity altogether, and very clearly a pure mother-goddess figure, represented in art with a multitude of breasts and sometimes with black features. She was widely worshipped in the Greek and Roman world, and the reference in the Bible (Acts XIX, 23–41) concerns a riot caused by an Ephesian silversmith called Demetrios who complained that St Paul's teachings, undermining the worship of Diana, were aimed at damaging his livelihood, which was based on making shrines and images of the goddess. This Diana specifically protected the city of Ephesus as well as having a wider currency as a fertility goddess.

Hera (the Roman Juno), who was the consort of Zeus, chief of the Graeco-Roman pantheon, was sometimes invoked as a protector in childbirth, and other goddesses often bear symbols of fruitfulness: Fortuna, for example, normally carries a cornucopia. Aphrodite (Venus) is also very definitely concerned with fertility, though her main association is with love and beauty. Her origins were quite separate in the Greek and Roman forms; in the latter, her earliest manifestation may have been as a spirit of fields and gardens, concerned more with the increase of plants than animals. Some local cults of Aphrodite, however, had a very specific sexual content: her temples at Corinth, at Paphos in Cyprus (Cyprus was, according to legend, the birthplace of the goddess) and at Eryx in Sicily all housed temple prostitutes whose services were dedicated to the goddess. It may be that echoes of some form of sacred prostitution are preserved even in depictions such as 23, a figure-type common on Gaulish samian pottery of the second century AD, which shows a couple with the woman apparently seated on an altar. Aphrodite was the patron goddess of the flourishing city of Corinth, which had a reputation in antiquity for its numerous, skilled and expensive courtesans.

It is in the Celtic areas of the Roman Empire that we find some of the most explicit mother-goddess images, and it is clear that these must express a romanisation of deities already important in the local Celtic population. Large stone sculptures dedicated to the three Matres or Matrones (mothers or matrons) are found in Gaul and Britain and the Rhineland; their triple nature underlines their Celtic origin, since triple manifestations of a deity are distinctive in Celtic

24 Bronze and marble figure of the Diana (Artemis) of Ephesus. 2nd century AD

belief. In Gaul there was a flourishing industry in the first and second centuries AD turning out small mould-made figurines in fine white pipe-clay: the most common subjects in a very large repertoire were a naked Venus and a goddess who was shown seated in a high-backed basket-work chair, suckling one or a pair of infants. These were probably relatively inexpensive statuettes for votive use, and it is fair to assume that they may have been bought chiefly by women, hence the emphasis on deities which had particular responsibility for feminine problems.

If we turn from mother-goddesses to the worship and rites of male fertility deities, we at once enter the realm of 'obscene' representations. On the whole, the use of the male sex organ alone as a symbol has a specific meaning connected not with any individual deity, but with the apotropaic power of the phallus itself, that is, its power to avert and overcome evil influences. Models of a phallus, often of impressive size, played a part in numerous religious rites, especially those connected with the worship of Dionysos, and we shall consider these further in a later chapter. A Greek example of the type of festival concerned is that of Haloa, which took place in ancient Athens in December, and was intended to ensure the successful germination and growth of the seed which was sown. The proceedings, carried out mainly by women, may have had a fairly orgiastic content, but included banquets at which foods in phallic form were consumed. This may well be the explanation of the decoration on a red-figure fragment which shows a girl holding a large, deep container full of eyed phalluses. Another interesting picture depicts a girl sprinkling model phalluses to help seed to grow (5). Hetairai apparently took part in this festival; the hetairai were the courtesans of Athens, a class socially quite distinct from the common prostitutes, and superior to them: another vase-painting (27) shows two of them dancing round an enormous phallus, undoubtedly in connection with a festival such as Haloa.

Many of the male deities who were concerned with fertility were of early and obscure origin, and even the writers of antiquity were forced to be vague and contradictory about them. Naturally, they share many characteristics with each other, including an affinity with animals, especially sheep and goats, their presence in country places, and the ability to terrify and awe humans. They were also accorded a protective role over property in general as well as flocks and crops, so that they are charged with the marking of property boundaries. Finally, they possessed the power to be malevolent if not propitiated, though they would keep away evil when properly respected. There are really no clear and sharp distinctions between some of the gods we shall consider here, and we must remember that there must have been many local versions of these basic fertility cults of which we know little or nothing. Many of these deities express their powers of fertility, at least on occasion, by being depicted in sexual situations or as ithyphallic, that is, with an erect penis. Whether such images were regarded with religious awe or with a sort of friendly amusement would depend on the place, the time, the god and the context, but they are all basically religious in function and intention, and to classify them as in any way obscene or licentious would be to misunderstand completely their meaning in their ancient context.

One of the best known of these basic nature gods is Pan, the Greek god of flocks and herds who was depicted in art as half-man, half-goat. The myths about Pan's parentage vary, but he was usually thought of as a son of Hermes. One of the few specific myths about him concerns his creation of the syrinx, or Pan-pipes, from

25 A Gaulish figurine moulded in white pipeclay. representing a mother-goddess seated in a basket-work chair, nursing a baby. This is a universally acceptable image of fertility. 2nd century AD

26 A sherd from a red-figure vase
showing a girl holding a container of eyed
phalluses. 5th century BC

27 Red-figure cup: the scene of hetairai
dancing round a model phallus is
connected with a religious festival.
5th century BC

reeds into which the nymph Syrinx had been transformed in order to escape his amorous attentions. Other stories attribute the invention of this musical instrument to Hermes himself. Pan was linked in other ways with music. He was seen as a shepherd god, ensuring the health and fertility of his charges, while his darker side included the ability to engender panic in men, the mysterious fear which can afflict humans in lonely country places. (The word 'panic' is derived from the name of the god.) This is another matter which it is easy for the modern town-dweller to despise and attribute to ignorance and superstition, but it is real enough.

The god Pan appears in some early Greek vase-paintings and statuettes with the head of a goat, but in Hellenistic and Roman times the standard image is of a human figure with goat's legs, horns and pointed ears and with facial features which, though coarse and animal-like, are basically human. The similarity of his overall appearance to that of the satyrs who form part of the entourage of Dionysos is obvious. Indeed, Pan also appeared as a plural god (Pans) and sometimes even as female, and was himself one of the companions of Dionysos, so inevitably by Roman times his original nature had blurred and broadened out a

28 A red-figure cup by the Brygos painter, showing satyrs attacking Hera, who is defended by Hermes and Hercules. 500–475 BC

29 Sherd from a bowl in Central Gaulish samian ware, with a figure-type of the god Pan. Early 2nd century AD

good deal. Furthermore, the Latin god Faunus, as we shall see, shared most of Pan's salient characteristics, though he does not appear to have had any of the physical attributes of a goat, and it is probable that in late antiquity Pan, Faunus and sundry fauns and satyrs were considered virtually identical. All were popular in decorative art at this time, and formed part of the Dionysiac (Bacchic) scenes which were greatly favoured.

One derivation of Pan's name, etymologically incorrect, connects it with the Greek for 'all' or 'everything', and there was therefore a current of thought which considered this god to be a universal deity. Though this is probably far from his original, more local function, it is worth mentioning that nature deities such as Pan represent a far deeper and more powerful stratum of religious belief than the formalised and humanised gods and goddesses of the central Graeco-Roman pantheon. It was the type of the horned, hoofed god which in medieval times was regarded as the personification of paganism, and thus the antithesis of Christian beliefs. The Christian concept of the Devil owes much to the idea of Pan, though it would be simplistic to suggest that they were one and the same.

Pan's concern with fertility is sometimes, though by no means always, expressed by depicting him as ithyphallic, or actually engaged in sexual activity. Probably the most famous version of the latter is the marble sculpture from

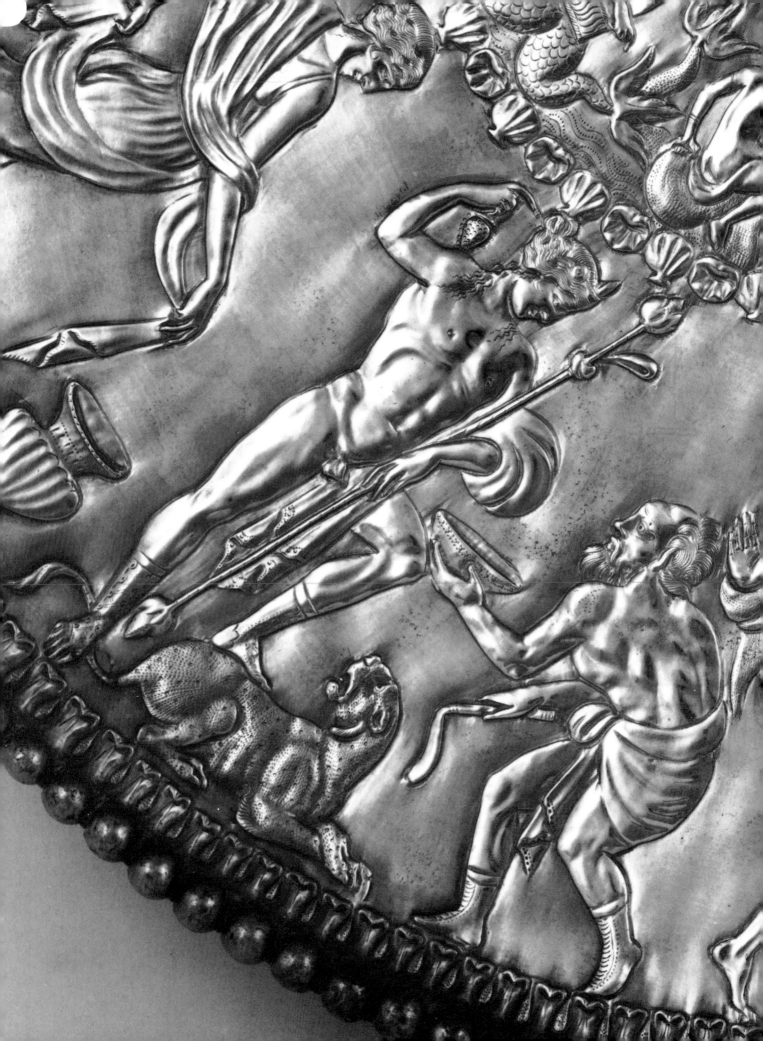

Herculaneum of Pan copulating with a she-goat (1). This is artistically an outstanding piece of work, and the combination of Pan's animal limbs and strangely non-human face with the unnaturally human posture of the goat makes a powerful statement on the mingling of human and animal in the personality of the god. It is this statue that became well known through engravings.

Pan is not infrequently depicted sexually accosting other deities, nymphs, shepherds and shepherdesses, and, as in the case of the satyrs, such scenes are often light-hearted and humorous; some, however, give an idea of the darker and more sinister side of the god, such as one red-figure scene which shows a fleeing youth who may be suffering from a real attack of panic. Pan features as a standard type even in the decoration of provincial Roman products such as samian ware – the figure type in 29 was in use in the first half of the second century and depicts a rather handsome ithyphallic version of the god. The pose of the figure has obviously been selected to ensure that the phallus is clearly visible; like the goat's legs and horns, it was seen as one of the distinguishing attributes of this deity. Even later, in the fourth century AD, Pans (in the plural) are often found decorating marble sarcophagi, where they form part of Bacchic scenes, and this theme is found also on the great silver dish from Mildenhall in Suffolk (16). The Mildenhall Pan is likewise taking part in Bacchic revels. He is a magnificent figure, powerful and dignified, not to be regarded as a comic or negligible rustic godling but as a serious and potent deity.

The link between Pan, who was of Greek origin, and Faunus, a god of Latium, the area south and east of Rome, has been mentioned above. Faunus is known primarily from literary sources and there is no clearly identifiable iconography for him. His worship is mentioned by major writers of the first centuries BC and AD, Livy, Horace, Virgil and Ovid. Many of his characteristics and powers are virtually the same as those of Pan, a god of fields and livestock, protecting his charges on the one hand and bringing them health and increase, while on the other hand capable of provoking terror and bringing harm and distress. The possible derivations of his name illuminate some of these concepts. Faunus may be derived from the verb *faveo*, to befriend or protect, which would give the meaning 'kindly' or 'propitious one'. This could be quite seriously meant as a descriptive title, but could also have an inner meaning intended to discourage the god from turning against his charges: flattering names were often given to potentially dangerous spirits in order to ensure that they would not exercise the darker side of their powers. One of the names given to the Furies of Greek myth was *Eumenides*, 'the well-disposed ones', while in later times, the Fairies, who, if displeased, could cause untold harm to livestock and to children, were propitiated with names like 'the good people', and in Welsh, *y tylwyth teg*, 'the fair folk'. Another possible source of the name Faunus embodies the verb *fari*, to speak, which would give the meaning 'seer' or 'foreteller'. Prophetic gifts and the ability to cause dreams, including nightmares, were also among his qualities. Just as Pan engendered panic, so Faunus was responsible for the strange and frightening noises which are sometimes heard in lonely country places. All in all, it is evident that the dividing line between Pan and Faunus is very hard to draw, at least by the late antique period. It may well be that representations which we interpret as depicting Pan might easily have been thought of as Faunus by those who created them, thus explaining the apparent scarcity of the iconographic evidence for Faunus.

5 *opposite* A detail of the decoration on a red-figure vase by the Hasselmann Painter, which shows a woman sprinkling phalluses set in the ground: the context is probably a fertility festival. c.430–420 BC

30 *previous page* A detail from the decoration of the great silver dish in the Mildenhall (Suffolk) treasure, which shows Bacchus and Silenus with dancing satyrs and maenads. 4th century AD

6 *left* Priapus, in a wall-painting from the House of the Vettii at Pompeii. He is standing by a large basket of fruit, and is engaged in weighing his phallus. 1st century AD

7 *right* A Roman wall-painting of a satyr and maenad, from Pompeii.

8 A mosaic panel from the House of the
Faun at Pompeii, depicting a young satyr
and a maenad. 2nd century BC

31 *right* Detail from a Roman marble
sarcophagus with Bacchic decoration,
including Pans, both male and female.
Second half of the 2nd century AD

32 Bronze statuette of Priapus anointing his phallus. 1st century AD

33 *above* Terracotta statuette of Priapus, with his cloak full of fruit. From Pompeii. 1st century BC–1st century AD

34 *opposite* Terracotta figurine from Pompeii of a Pan or faun with an exaggerated phallus. This was possibly a hanging lamp. 1st century AD

Statuettes which are thought to represent Faunus depict a bearded and solemn god wearing a goatskin, but without the actual goat-like features of Pan. Indeed, there is a further confusion here in that yet another important rustic deity, Silvanus, is similarly represented, and like Pan and Faunus, has protective and fertility-bringing functions. There is no suggestion that Faunus was ever shown as ithyphallic, unless some of the Roman Pan images are really Faunus, but he was nevertheless a god of fecundity and may well have been the deity venerated at the Roman festival of the Lupercalia, as well as being worshipped at various local feasts. The Lupercalia embodied both fertility aspects and the idea of marking and securing the boundaries of a territory. As we shall see with Hermes and Silvanus, this is another common side of the duties of gods concerned with fertility. According to Livy, a temple to Faunus was built in Rome on the Tiber island and was dedicated on 13 February 194 BC, two days before the Lupercalia. By the time of the late Republic and the early Empire, the origins of this festival were already obscure, and there is no certainty that Faunus was the god invoked, though both ancient and modern authorities have tended to assume that he was. The feast itself involved the sacrifice of a goat and a dog, and after various rites had been performed naked youths ran through the city with thongs made from the skin of the slaughtered goat: women who were barren would become fertile if struck by these. Another facet of the worship of Faunus is that a female form, Fauna, may have been identical with the Bona Dea, the Good Goddess. Her worship was an exclusively female cult in Rome, and though the rites were secret, there can be little doubt that fertility was a basic aspect of it.

Pagan religion continued to flourish after the establishment of Christianity as the official religion of the Roman Empire in the fourth century AD. The worship of Faunus, specifically, was deprecated by the Christian writer Arnobius early in that century, and archaeological evidence for the cult of Faunus at the end of the fourth century emerged most unexpectedly in 1979 when a treasure of jewellery and spoons was found near Thetford, Norfolk. The silver spoons bear inscriptions referring to Faunus, combining his name with Celtic, i.e. Gaulish or British, names or epithets. This demonstrates that the local Latian god mentioned by authors of the early Empire was still venerated in relatively far-flung areas of the Empire in the late fourth century, though what rites marked his worship remains unknown to us. It seems certain that a ritual meal was involved, but it is also highly likely that feasts of Faunus would, at least at some times and places, have had a somewhat orgiastic character. Nevertheless, as we have already seen, there is no evidence that Faunus himself was ever depicted as an ithyphallic deity.

A deity who was always phallic, on the other hand, was Priapus, another early fertility god. His particular responsibility lay with the fertility of gardens and farms, and statues of him, often quite crudely carved in wood, were apparently a common feature of the countryside. Priapus was thought to be a son of Dionysos, though there are varying myths about his origin. Iconographically, he appears as a somewhat grotesque figure with a grossly exaggerated and erect penis; his garment is often drawn up to reveal this remarkable organ, and the folds of cloth contain fruit, to demonstrate his function of ensuring the increase of crops. There are a number of Roman representations, for example from Pompeii, which depict him anointing his phallus with oil (32), and there is a famous painting from the House of the Vettii at Pompeii (6) in which he is weighing his phallus on a scales. A statue of Priapus protected property as well as bringing about fertility, and in

35 A Hellenistic bronze statuette of Priapus, his responsibility for fertility symbolised here by four infants supported in his cloak, rather than the more usual fruit.

36 *opposite* A red-figure cup by Epiktetos, which illustrates a sculptor in the process of making a herm. Last quarter of the 6th century BC

this his function approaches that of certain manifestations of Hermes, as well as Pan, Faunus and Silvanus. In Roman times, Priapus seems to have been regarded with amusement and affection rather than awe, though this would not have prevented him from being propitiated in an appropriate manner, with gifts of the first-fruits of the land over which he watched.

The emphasis on the phallus itself in the statues of Priapus links him with the use of the phallus alone as a protective and apotropaic device, which we shall consider more closely in the next chapter. Ensuring fertility is closely bound up with protection: to achieve health and increase, dangerous pests, diseases and harmful weather have to be warded off. The power of the phallus to drive away evil influences is therefore one with its obvious symbolism of promoting reproduction. At the same time, the artistic evidence implies that over-large male genitals were considered aesthetically unpleasing by the Greeks and Romans. Pan and the satyrs are often generously endowed in this respect, but they were seen as partly animal; the ideal type of male beauty epitomised in classical sculpture, Greek and Roman, normally depicts genitals of somewhat less than the average size for the racial type concerned, certainly never more. Consequently, the exaggerated genitals of Priapus made him seem an ugly and grotesque figure, though benevolent.

Priapus as depicted in the somewhat mannered style of Roman early imperial art at Pompeii has a certain style and elegance in spite of this, but it is likely that the rustic wooden statuettes would have been very simple, and may well have approximated in appearance the ancient type of the herm. Herms were an aspect of the god Hermes (Mercury), though herms of other deities also occur and, indeed, herms of non-divine characters. The herm was a boundary-marker, protecting land and possessions, and was common to both Greek and Roman culture, though its function became perhaps less religious and more purely decorative as time went on. It took the form of a head carved in the round surmounting a simple angular pillar, on the front of which was added a set of male genitals, usually erect. The concept almost certainly developed from simple stones which were used as boundary markers and identified with Hermes as a protective deity. In Greece herms were treated with great reverence. There are many scenes on painted pottery which show them being crowned or garlanded, or presented with offerings. One of the well-known incidents of Athenian history was the mutilation of the city herms in 415 BC, as a result of which the brilliant young leader Alkibiades, suspected of involvement in the act of desecration, fell from popular favour.

Herms continue to occur as a type in the Roman period, though it is doubtful if their significance is as great; figure types representing either herms or statues of Priapus occur on Arretine and samian pottery in the first and second centuries AD (38). It is possible that at this date there may be some conflation between Hermes in this form and Priapus.

A great body of myth surrounds Hermes himself, who is approximately equivalent to the Roman god Mercury and holds an important position in the official Graeco-Roman pantheon, yet he, again, shares some of the basic traits of Pan, Faunus and the like. Hermes was a son of Zeus, and from birth showed the enterprise and cunning that made him the patron of commerce and even of theft. He was a god of travellers and the messenger of the gods, equipped for travelling in his cloak and broad-brimmed traveller's hat (*petasos*) and sandals, and carrying a

53

37 *above* A small bronze herm of Cupid from Pompeii. 1st century AD

38 *above right* Figure of a herm depicted on Arretine ware. Late 1st century BC

39 *opposite* Bronze statuette of the god Mercury with numerous phalluses and attachment rings for bells. 1st century AD

herald's staff, the *caduceus*. His speed is symbolised by the wings on his heels and sometimes his hat as well. The caduceus is generally shown entwined with two snakes and is sometimes winged. Another usual attribute carried by the god is a purse. Cockerels and tortoises are associated with Hermes, and so is the goat or ram, stressing his link with the shepherd deities already discussed. Except in the form of herms, he is not normally depicted as ithyphallic, and the bronze from Pompeii (39) is rather exceptional, but there is no doubt that this important deity is part of the group of male fertility gods concerned with agriculture and stockraising.

Hermes was widely venerated, and was a particularly popular deity in the Celtic provinces, probably because many of his characteristics corresponded with those of native gods. Silvanus, whom we have already mentioned several times, is also attested archaeologically as a god worshipped in the more distant Celtic areas of the Roman Empire as well as Italy. He was a god of Italian origin and, like Hermes, Priapus and Faunus, had special protective power over property boundaries and influenced the fertility of animals. Indeed, nearly all his characteristics can be precisely paralleled in those of Faunus. He was sometimes plural – Silvani – and could be a hostile and dangerous force as well as a kindly one.

There are also some major deities of the pantheon concerned with fertility and sexual matters. Eros (Cupid), the son of Aphrodite, is one of these. In Greek mythology Eros is the personification of physical, sexual love, and is represented as a beautiful youth. He was not invariably regarded as the child of Aphrodite: there are various versions of his origin, in some of which he is seen as one of the most ancient spirits, with no known parentage. By Hellenistic times the concept of this deity was changing, and in Roman times he is seen as a mischievous young boy, playing tricks on people and wounding them with his arrows, an image which survives into much later times. There were certain centres where Eros was especially venerated, and clearly there must have been a sexual element in his worship. Like so many important deities, he had a dark as well as a light side; sexual passion can be a cruel and unrewarding experience.

Dionysos or Bacchus, the god of wine, has already been mentioned in connection with Pan and the satyrs who formed part of his retinue. He was a god of very great importance, and deeply concerned with fertility; the rites connected with his worship grew up into the ancient theatre, and we shall look at him, and the images to which his worship gave rise, in far greater detail later on.

Even this most superficial survey should give some idea of the importance of fertility deities in Greek and Roman religion. We know of only a few of the rites which this worship engendered, and though to our sensibilities it may seem perfectly extraordinary to dance round a huge model phallus or to hang garlands on a phallic pillar, we know that these things were done in all seriousness by ordinary people, for reasons which were not connected with personal pleasure in sexual activity. To categorise as obscene images connected with worship of a deep and solemn kind is an irrelevant reaction. We might remember, too, that our reactions depend very much on just how explicit a symbol is. Only the most severely puritanical Christian condemns the country dance round the maypole, though this may be as much for its pagan origin as its sexual implications.

The religious objects and concepts mentioned so far are all linked with gods and cults which could help to ensure fertility and good fortune. There is another and slightly different field of religious practice in antiquity which could and did give rise to objects which were disturbing to later puritan minds. The custom of presenting gifts to a god at his shrine or temple, either in the hope of receiving favours from the deity or in gratitude for favours already received was an ancient one, widespread in the classical world. Divine help and guidance was sought for everything from affairs of state to the most commonplace domestic problems. Illness was naturally one of the troubles referred to supernatural powers, and certain deities had special competence in such matters. Of the major gods and goddesses, Apollo and Minerva were most often charged with healing, and certain shrines were associated with them in this role. As we have already seen, several goddesses could be invoked to help women in childbirth and disorders arising from it. There were also deities whose prime function was healing; undoubtedly, many of these would have been local spirits, but one or two had cults widespread in the Graeco-Roman world, notably Asclepius, represented in art as a kindly, bearded figure, and his daughter Hygieia, who personified health and was equated with the Latin Salus. The most important cult centre of Asclepius was at Epidauros in Greece, but a temple was built for him in Rome, on the Tiber island, as early as the third century BC.

The choice of particular places for the growth of healing shrines and the worship of healing deities was naturally connected with the special properties of those places, very often the presence of mineral springs. Sources of water were venerated by most early societies, and when the water had some unusual characteristic, such as heat, effervescence, or minerals which imparted a noticeable taste, the source was well fitted to develop into a holy place. During the Roman occupation of Britain, for example, the hot springs at Bath were honoured by elaborate buildings, and the name of the deity of the place, Sulis Minerva, is that mixture of Celtic and Latin which demonstrates that the site was already a holy one to the Celts. Shrines such as those to Asclepius which were based on sources of healing water appear in many cases to have grown up to resemble the great spas of the nineteenth century or the modern German *Kurort*, offering accommodation for the worshippers/patients, the services of medical

40 The magnificent theatre of Epidauros. Through the trees to the right lay the buildings which made up the sanctuary of Asclepius.

practitioners, and facilities for exercise and dieting. Some healing shrines would undoubtedly have specialised in the treatment of particular types of illness, while others may have been more general, relying simply on the nature of the god to deal with whatever problems the supplicants brought him. There is every reason to believe that shrines of this kind could often have played an important part in the alleviation or cure of many ailments. Mineral waters can be very efficaceous in the treatment of some conditions, and allied with the power of faith, and with medical advice and treatment, there must have been many who had reason to dedicate a thank-offering to the god before they left.

All ancient temple sites offered various ancillary services, and these would generally have included stalls selling suitable *ex votos*, gifts for the worshipper to present to the god. These votive offerings can take many forms; they can be in the form of actual money, of other valuable items such as jewellery, of metal plaques inscribed with a suitable invocation, or of statuettes in various materials – bronze, the cheaper terracotta, and probably also less durable substances such as wood. Votives connected with physical disorders could take the form of models of the afflicted parts of the body. This custom was found only sporadically, but appears to have been especially common in Italy in the period of the Roman Republic. Some examples of anatomical *ex votos* made of terracotta from Italy are illustrated in 41 to 44. Parts of the body frequently figured are the eyes, head, hands, breasts, male genitals, legs and feet. Some internal organs are also found, particularly wombs, while complete statuettes of animals presumably indicate an appeal for help with the illnesses of domestic beasts. The precise interpretation of the parts of the body in terms of what diseases were common, is very difficult. The subject is discussed by the late Calvin Wells in a section of T. W. Potter's paper on the healing shrine at Ponte di Nona. The prevalence of a particular part of the body at any given sanctuary could indicate that the shrine had a good reputation

in the healing of diseases afflicting that part, so that sufferers attended it from a wide radius. On the other hand, it could also indicate that disorders of that part of the body were especially common in that area, or were an especially serious disability in that particular community. At Ponte di Nona feet are very common votives, and Dr Wells makes the point that in a rural community such as that surrounding that site, injuries or afflictions of the feet and legs would be particularly serious, preventing those who were engaged in the heavy physical work of farming from moving around to earn their living.

The relevance of this matter of healing shrines to our present purpose turns on the fact that terracotta models of the male genitals were common votives at certain shrines and, as antiquities, have been collected and often been categorised as 'obscene' in the past. It should be clear from the account above that the purpose of these is no more obscene than is that of a diagram in a medical textbook: they are intended simply to draw the attention of the deity to the part requiring help. Breasts and wombs are not readily considered indecent subjects, and votive models of the female external genitalia appear to be far less common than the male, suggesting that the gynaecological problems for which help was most often invoked concerned fertility, birth and the nourishment of infants, rather than troubles which directly affect the genital region, such as gonorrhoea or the minor, but nonetheless distressing, infections like monilia. Gonorrhoea can give rise to a more general infection which can result in sterility, so the precise inferences to be drawn from the organs presented as votives remain very unclear: certainly we cannot attempt to say with any certainty how common any condition was in a given area without a lot more evidence than we yet have.

Some of the examples of terracotta male genitals from Ponte di Nona may show evidence of the condition called phimosis, a tightness of the foreskin which can lead to painful and unpleasant consequences, though its surgical treatment is very straightforward. One of the results can be impotence, about the only cause of infertility for which the female partner can obviously not be held responsible; the concept of a male who is sexually competent yet infertile is not an easy one to accept in the absence of microscopes and the resultant knowledge of the existence of spermatozoa, though stockbreeders must have known from early times that some male animals rarely if ever impregnated the females. Some of these terracottas, therefore, may be concerned with our old theme of fertility. Others may imply sufferers from troubles of the urinary system, a very common type of affliction among older men.

All the material which we have considered in this chapter formed an important aspect of the religious practices and beliefs of ancient society. Earlier antiquaries were naturally perfectly well aware of the religious connotations of many 'indecent' representations, as evidenced by work such as Richard Payne Knight's, but it would still have been impossible until quite recent times to display or discuss an *ex voto* in the form of a penis in the same way as one in the form of a foot. Such a distinction is academically invalid, and even if we prefer to give special treatment to the overtly sexual categories of ancient imagery, such as those we shall discuss in later chapters, there can be no excuse for dealing thus with images which are related to religious practice, the understanding of which is absolutely crucial to our understanding of ancient society.

41–44 The terracotta *ex votos* (*opposite*), all dating from the third to the second century BC, would have been dedicated by worshippers at a healing shrine. These examples take the form of a hand (41), a female breast (42), male genitals (43), and a muscular internal organ, usually interpreted as a uterus (44).

3
The phallus
and the Evil Eye

We have seen that ithyphallic spirits like Priapus and the herms had a protective role which developed naturally and logically from their fertility-bringing functions. At the same time, basic nature gods of this kind could also have hostile and aggressive aspects, exemplified by the abilities of Pan, Silvanus and Faunus to frighten and harm people: any honest personification of natural forces must include cruelty as well as kindness. The essential and central power of such nature deities could conveniently be symbolised by the phallus alone, and this symbol would then take on something of the dual nature of the original god, protective on the one hand, and aggressive, perhaps dangerous, on the other. The phallus can thus become an apotropaic device in its own right, and was used as such in both Greek and Roman times, perhaps particularly the latter. Representations of the male genitals as small portable amulets and as carvings and paintings constitute an important class of material which many earlier students of antiquity unhesitatingly classed as indecent. In their own time such objects were regarded as good-luck charms; their significance was not erotic, any more than the medical *ex votos* described in the previous chapter. It would probably be wrong to imagine that phallic amulets were regarded with solemn religious awe, but they were more than the trivially superstitious charms which are popular today. Perhaps they could be classed somewhere between the wearing of a cross by a serious Christian and the primarily decorative four-leaved clover, black cat and the number 1 3 of modern times.

The use of the male genitals as a charm was greatly facilitated by the fact that they are easy to represent in simple and stylised form, divorced from the rest of the human figure, without becoming too ambiguous. It is true that the basic shape of the phallus is echoed in many other objects, both man-made and natural, and this undoubtedly confuses the issue when phallic symbolism or phallic worship are considered in general terms. However, this is less of a problem when Greek and Roman art is the subject of study, because of the literalness of art in those cultures. Many cultures other than the classical, from primitive societies to highly sophisticated ones, have afforded the phallus respect, amounting sometimes to worship. The enthusiastic and imaginative observer can find plenty of conscious and unconscious phallic imagery in the most unlikely places. In such cases it can become difficult to establish the source of the phallic symbolism – whether its alleged presence affords an insight into the society which gave rise to the art concerned, into the subconscious of the individual artist, or indeed into the subconscious of the observer. There must be many cases of phallic significance being thrust upon some innocent subject, but since the subconscious can always be made to take the responsibility a reliable judgement upon the matter is hard to make. Almost any protuberant or pointing object can be regarded with a knowing eye: some good examples occur in G. Ryley Scott's book *Phallic Worship*, where amongst other things the tall pointed towers of early medieval Ireland are regarded as specifically phallic. No doubt any tower, spire or other upstanding feature may be interpreted in this way, but this does not necessarily mean that the builders had any such thing in mind when they built a tall structure rather than a squat one; just one of several more obvious explanations is that defence might require a high point from which to scan the surrounding countryside. It is perhaps fair to point out that misinterpretation of the opposite kind can occur: the author remembers a disbelieving friend of hers persuasively arguing that the somewhat worn and stylised phallus carved on Roman masonry at the fort of

Birdoswald, on Hadrian's Wall, could perfectly well depict a pair of shears.

I do not intend to throw scorn at the idea that ambiguous representations of phallic forms occur, and may have considerable significance, but this happens most where the society cannot tolerate overt depiction of the object – which is the case in most Christian societies – or where the prevailing form of visual art is symbolically orientated, fond of double meanings, and scorning directness. On the whole, the graphic art of ancient Greece and Rome is straightforwardly figurative, and this, combined with a lack of nervousness about nudity and actual sexual matters, results in unambiguous images. When a classical artist or craftsman needed to represent a phallus, he could do so, and though the result might be simplified and stylised it would be recognisable. Consequently, it seems to me quite unnecessary to search for hidden phallic symbols in classical art.

Notwithstanding what has been said above, it is true that during the Roman Empire, one of the great art styles which encountered and mingled with that of Rome was the art of the Celts, a supreme example of abstract, symbolic and non-representational art in antiquity. Celtic art appears to have practically no demonstrable erotic or sexual content, and any phallic symbolism which it may contain is very hard to demonstrate as intentional. It is a very striking and important fact that it is under the influence of Roman artistic convention that these aspects start to appear: this is what Hermet was complaining of – the wicked corruption by the Romans of his ancestors, the Gauls (pp. 32–3).

The range of objects in the Graeco-Roman world which could be made in the form of the male genitals, or decorated with them, was wide. The simple phallus, made of bronze, brass, bone, or even gold, and worn as an amulet, or the carving in bas-relief on a wall, is characteristic of Roman culture rather than Greek, and is very common. Greek representations like those on painted cups are usually associated with other scenes or objects, but their significance remains apotropaic.

As an amulet to be worn on the person, some of the most charming are the tiny gold finger-rings (10). These have a minute phallus in relief on the bezel. The rings are far too small even to have been worn on the most slender adult finger, and if worn as rings at all they must have belonged to very young children. Alternatively, they could have been worn on a chain as a pendant. It seems likely that they were intended to protect and bring good luck to small children of the class able and permitted to wear gold jewellery: children, even of privileged classes, are very vulnerable to accident and disease, and a protective amulet must have seemed a sensible precaution.

Also in the class of high-quality and expensive jewellery are the small gold and coral pendants (10). The modern Italian pendants, usually of coral (or coral-coloured plastic) with a pointed, sinuous form, are distant descendants of these, made less explicit and more symbolic by the demands of a more shockable society. It has been suggested that the rare Roman bronze pendants of a not dissimilar form are also phallic symbols, but because it was acceptable to wear a realistic representation of a phallus, this seems most unlikely. If these are phallic at all, they probably represent the male organ of an animal, for example a boar, and thus combine the apotropaic function with the power and virility symbolism associated with many animals. The wearing of a phallus amulet round the neck is mentioned by Varro (*de lingua latina*, VII, 97) and its apotropaic function clearly indicated; it is worn by boys, 'to prevent harm from coming to them'.

Other simple phallic pendants are made from copper alloys – bronze and brass –

45 A Roman phallic amulet carved from a section of red-deer antler.

46 A phallus as a good-luck symbol in mosaic at the threshold of a Roman house in Ostia, the port of Rome.

9 *opposite* A terracotta figurine, made at Myrina (Turkey) of a woman crowning a herm of Dionysos. Late 2nd century BC

or bone, and it is not always clear which are intended for human use and which are harness-trappings for horses. In either case, they are designed to ensure safety and good fortune, rather than actual fertility, for the wearer. Those which are carved on a cross-section of red deer antler are quite common on military sites in the northern provinces of the Roman Empire, and the choice of material is interesting in itself. Not only does a section of antler provide a very suitable base for such a carving, being easily available, free and producing a neat, disc-shaped pendant with a naturally decorative edge, but the association with the red deer stag in itself may add power to the object. Any large, strong male animal tends to be admired for its apparent fighting and sexual prowess, and beasts such as stags, bulls, boars and stallions are of considerable importance in the religious beliefs of many peoples of antiquity. The Celtic population of Rome's northerly provinces were among these, and included antlered and horned deities among their complex and now imperfectly understood pantheon. The antlered god, who is named on one Gaulish inscription as Cernunnos, was depicted from time to time in pre-Roman and Romano-Celtic art, while a triple-horned bull also occurs in Gaulish statuettes, sometimes associated with other deities. Boars were also venerated, and images of them were common in the Celtic provinces during the Empire as well as earlier. In Roman provincial contexts boar's-tusk amulets are well known. They are probably not phallic in any sense, but the connection with a boar gives them adequate symbolism in themselves.

Simple phalluses were displayed not only as personal good-luck charms but also in a more public way, on walls, floors, buildings and so on. These are not casual graffiti, but carefully executed apotropaic devices. It is noticeable that they tend to be displayed at places of potential danger, such as corners, bridges and entrances. Naturally, the greatest variety of examples survives from Pompeii and Herculaneum, but many are known from elsewhere, and they must have been a familiar feature in Roman life. The carefully carved example illustrated in *12* is from high up on a wall at a street corner in Pompeii. Another famous example from the same town is carved rather crudely on a panel of travertine, and bears an inscription, *hic habitat felicitas* ('here dwells happiness'). While this may have been a 'shop sign', indicating that the building housed prostitutes, it is more likely that it was a normal protective symbol, strengthened and reinforced by the accompanying phrase. Another phallus, very worn, is known on a paving stone from Pompeii, and further examples represented on floors include a fine one done in black and white mosaic on the threshold of a building in the Italian harbour town of Ostia (46), and a small mosaic example, decorated with a bell, a feature to which we shall return, on the floor of a room in the women's public baths at Herculaneum.

Walls and bath-houses were adorned in this way not only in Italy, but also in the most distant provinces of the Empire. The phallus on a wall at Birdoswald has been mentioned; there is another good example tucked away low on the Roman bridge-abutment at Chesters, Northumberland, and another in the military bath-house at the same site. Bath-houses were especially in need of this type of protection: not only were men felt to be particularly vulnerable when unclothed, but it was also common for games of chance to be played in the relaxing and sociable surroundings of the bath. Good luck was needed to ensure that one did not altogether lose the shirt one had already removed.

In addition to the rings and pendants mentioned above, the phallus occurs as a

11 An engraved carnelian gem depicting
Hercules and Omphale. Second half of the
1st century BC

10 *left* A group of small items of Roman
jewellery in gold and coral, all making use
of phallic motifs as good-luck symbols.

12 *right* A carved panel from a wall at a
Pompeii street corner. The phallus is to
ward off danger. Roman, 1st century AD

13 *far left* A Roman bronze apotropaic ornament, a tintinnabulum, in phallic form.

14 *left* A bronze tintinnabulum in the form of a gladiator attacking an animal, which is also his own phallus. 1st century BC – 1st century AD

47 *right* A small wall-panel of travertine from Pompeii, carved for good luck with a phallus and the phrase *hic habitat felicitas* ('here dwells happiness').

48 A tiny enamelled bronze stud in the form of a phallus from the site of the Roman temple to Mercury at Uley, Gloucestershire. 2nd–3rd century AD

49 Painted Chian pottery phallus with an eye painted on the glans. Late 7th century BC

decorative motif on other items of wear and use, ranging from lamps and other pottery to enamelled brooches and seal-box lids. Items such as horse-brasses and jewellery made of enamelled bronze are very typical of the northern provinces, where there was a good Celtic tradition in the craft of enamelwork. Brooches and studs in the shapes of animals – hares, dogs, lions, birds, horses and dolphins, for instance – were well known, brightened with enamel inlay in red, green, blue, yellow and white. The little stud from a late Roman temple at Uley, Gloucestershire (48) illustrates how this technique creates a pretty and amusing trinket even in the form of a phallus.

We have looked so far at straightforward depictions of the male genitals alone, but not all phallic good-luck charms are so simple. The symbol is often accompanied by some other motif, to make its apotropaic function even more explicit; alternatively, the phallus may itself be elaborated into some fanciful form, personified into a fantastic independent little creature, or used as the central theme of a complex decorated object.

The first specific association of a phallus with another object which comes to mind is that of the phallus and an eye or pair of eyes. The Greek cups, like that in 76, illustrate the association very clearly. Eyes are themselves a charm against the Evil Eye: 'eye' beads, in blue and white glass, are still made in the Middle East with precisely this apotropaic function. The phallus, having a special power against the Evil Eye as well, makes a doubly powerful charm. It is often completely ambiguous in cases where both eyes and phallus are represented, whether the phallus is supposed to be overpowering the Evil Eye, or whether the eye motif is itself performing an apotropaic function. In some instances, the eye is definitely a personification of evil, and is clearly being attacked by the phallus. There are versions where the phallus is itself provided with eyes. This has been naively explained by suggesting that the phallus needs to be able to seek out its way, but in fact these eyes, like those painted on the prows of boats both in antiquity and modern times, are for luck and safety rather than direction-finding. There is a somewhat fragmentary example of a Greek pottery phallus of the seventh century BC in the British Museum (49) which has eyes painted on its glans. It was once mistaken, by some short-sighted or pure-minded scholar, for a boat.

There may well be some complications in the eye-and-phallus motifs over and above the understanding of the Evil Eye concept itself. Some psychologists regard eyes and genitals (both male and female) as being significantly related: the many myths in which blinding is the punishment for the breaking of sexual taboos, such as the story of Oedipus, are said to have a deep-seated basis in human psychology. In very recent times, blindness was supposed to be the ultimate and just punishment for the sexual 'crime' of masturbation, and this was earnestly believed. It was presumably easy enough to 'prove' by demonstrating that practically everybody who went blind in later life had at some time indulged in masturbation. Another complication arises in the interpretation of some of the simpler and more stylised representations in which eyes and phalluses occur. The problem of depicting the female genitals will be discussed below, but it may be touched on here; a simple elliptical shape in association with a likewise much stylised phallus could, in some instances, depict a vulva, and not an eye at all. This could entirely change the meaning, or it could even on occasion be a deliberate visual ambiguity. One of the most explicit and remarkable representations of the power of the phallus over the Evil Eye is an extraordinary small terracotta of

50 Red-figure vase by the Flying-angel Painter: the scene is of a girl holding a phallus-bird and uncovering a basket of phalluses. 500–475 BC

Hellenistic or Roman date (51), which shows a pair of phalluses, personified into complete little individuals, sawing in half a large eye which lies between them.

The phallus used as a protective device in buildings was elaborated into more consciously decorative forms than the simple carvings on walls which we have already seen. Mobiles, made of bronze and hung with bells, were intended for hanging up in the open courtyard of a house, where the wind would move them and make them tinkle. Bells themselves help to ward off evil, and clearly their effect could be strengthened if the mobile incorporated some other apotropaic

51 A terracotta figurine depicting two personified phalluses sawing an eye in half: a symbol of the power of the phallus over the Evil Eye. 1st century BC

motif as well. Consequently, these mobiles, known as *tintinnabula* from the presence of the bells, very often include phallic forms. Examples are known from many sites in the Roman Empire, some of the finest examples surviving from Pompeii.

Among the examples illustrated here (52, 54), it is striking to note how often animals become part of the design, or the phalluses themselves are transformed into animals by the addition of legs, tails, wings, and even ears (52). A tintinnabulum from Pompeii which depicts a gladiator attacking a beast, a dog or wolf, is particularly interesting, as this ravening monster is in fact the gladiator's own phallus. It is not at all certain whether this expresses a fear of sexuality as an uncontrollable animal urge, or whether it is simply intended to be startling or amusing. The feeling of anxiety about the power of sexuality certainly existed in antiquity, as we shall see in the discussion of the satyrs and similar beings, and their place in mythology.

The addition of legs and wings to phalluses may express two or three different concepts. Firstly, transforming the phallus into a small independent animal may stress the independent nature of the organ, often very much less under its owner's control than he might wish. Secondly, the power of the phallus is underlined by associating and even almost conflating it, not only with the deities we have already mentioned, such as Priapus, but also with certain animals which were supposed to be well endowed with sexual vigour and general vitality. A wide

52 *opposite* A very fine Roman bronze tintinnabulum, said to have been found in the River Mosel at Trier. *c.* 1st century AD

53 A small bronze amulet in the form of a
phallus-bird, with wings, tail and bird's
legs. Roman.

range of creatures, ranging from goats and dogs to domestic fowl and other birds,
were credited with particularly licentious habits. Rather curiously, the cat does
not seem to be included, though it would seem an obvious candidate, with its
frequent and abandoned sexual behaviour; cats were relatively uncommon as
domestic animals or pets in antiquity. A terracotta in the Trier museum shows a
dog-phallus sitting in typically canine fashion, while winged examples, with or
without bird or mammal legs, are very common. In both Latin and modern Italian
words for 'bird' or 'sparrow' occur as slang terms for the penis. Animal-phalluses
often engage in activities connected neither with sex nor the averting of evil
influences, for example, the chariot-pulling phalluses on a Romano-British pot
(78). In this area, it becomes difficult to disentangle purely apotropaic purposes
from entertainment.

As one might expect from the occasionally phallic nature of the god Mercury,
the ram, one of his attributes, is sometimes connected with phallic symbolism; a
bronze tintinnabulum from Pompeii depicts Mercury seated astride an ithyphallic
ram. The animal is provided with a decidedly human phallus. Another famous
example is the multi-phallic Mercury from Pompeii (39), which would originally
have been provided with bells depending from his numerous projections. This
extraordinary figure has a phallus in the usual place, together with an additional
four, plus the normal pair of wings, on his hat. He carries his usual attribute of a
purse, but the caduceus (with its own faint phallic connotations) is missing.
Together with the bells, this would have been a formidably apotropaic object, but
one cannot help feeling that its original owner must have found it pleasantly
amusing as well.

54 *opposite* A bronze tintinnabulum from
Pompeii: the ram is one of the animals
which normally accompanies the god
Mercury. Here the deity is riding the ram,
and the apotropaic effect of the object is
stressed by the fact that the latter is
ithyphallic. 1st century AD

The personification of phalluses into complete beings can include humans as well as animals. The terracotta depicting the destruction of the Evil Eye is one example, since presumably only humans could be expected to use a saw. There is a small human-legged phallus in bronze in the Boston museum, and there are some statuettes of a minor deity who wears a hooded cloak which lifts off to reveal a phallus instead of a head. These are found in Celtic provinces, and are a reminder that the hooded 'duffle-coat' was a typical garment of the cool, damp north. The association of head and phallus can be found in other amulets, where it seems that the two together may represent the whole essence of a figure, as in the herms.

Perhaps one may suggest an interpretation in which the higher and lower aspects of humanity are combined, and the cerebral and animal powers are symbolised by these two members. There may even be more to it than that. We have often noted that Celtic art is highly symbolic, and the head, frequently a disembodied, severed head, plays a very important role in Celtic mythology and art. Whether it may even have some phallic significance itself is debatable, but in any case, in a Celtic province of Rome, there can be no doubt that an amulet which combined the force of a head and a phallus would be powerful against evil.

Another small group of amulets exists in which the phallus is combined with a hand, usually making a gesture which is taken to be a sexually significant one. On this subject, we must turn to the matter of the representation of the female genitals, which at first sight seems to be conspicuously lacking in both Greek and Roman contexts. The point has already been made that the female genitals do not lend themselves so well to artistic depiction as the male, particularly in line rather than in three-dimensional media. I am speaking here of the vulva itself, rather than the pubes, or mons veneris, which is too featureless a form to be artisitically useful. The vulva is rarely seen: its situation makes it invisible in any normal position even to its owner, and visible to another only in a consciously arranged and specifically sexual pose. In contrast, the male genitals are visible in most positions in a state of undress. The full complexity of the female genitals lies, of course, in their totally invisible internal structure, but even when revealed, the vulva is artistically an inconvenient and ill-defined shape, lacking the clear and characteristic outlines of the male organs which makes it possible to draw or model them as a completely detached unit. There is also a considerable range of variability in the appearance of the external genitals between women of different ages, and as most people, even in antiquity, have not seen very many, even a faithfully realistic representation can look quite odd and improbable. The structure of the labia and clitoris is difficult to reproduce in three dimensions, and exceptionally ambiguous when drawn in simple outline. All in all, from the technical point of view alone, there is a strong case for representing the female genitals symbolically rather than realistically.

Setting aside for the moment the suitability or otherwise of the female genitalia for graphic portrayal, we should consider whether they are likely to fulfil the same role as an apotropaic symbol as does the phallus. The answer to this is complicated by the fact that one is dealing, in classical antiquity as now, with a male-dominated society. Psychologists consider that the female genitals, as symbols of female power and mystery, can appear dangerous and threatening: this is fairly difficult for a female to envisage, to whom the phallus appears a far more threatening and potentially harmful concept, but it may well be true, at

55 A bronze phallic pendant in partly human form. Roman.

56 *above* A Roman bone amulet combining the apotropaic powers of the phallus and the *mano fica* gesture.

57 *right* A complex Roman bronze amulet of a well-known type, incorporating three lucky symbols, the hand, phallus and crescent.

least on occasion. As an aggressive and powerful symbol, it would be reasonable to expect the vulva to be used at times to frighten away harmful forces, though perhaps it would cause more anxiety in (male) observers than the phallus. Careful observation suggests that it was indeed used thus from time to time.

We have already seen that in some examples of a phallus and 'eye' the latter could equally well be a simplified rendering of a vulva. The interpretation of this is very ambiguous indeed: the vulva could on the one hand be reinforcing the statement of the phallus, increasing its power against the Evil Eye, or then again, it could itself be taking the role of the Evil Eye, and be depicted as a power which is conquered and overcome by the phallus. Perhaps more definite are those amulets which depict, either alone or in conjunction with a phallus, a hand making a specific gesture (57) in which the fingers are curled and the thumb thrust between the index and middle fingers. This gesture has survived into modern times, and like so many ancient and powerful symbols, can have quite contradictory meanings. In some areas it is regarded as a good-luck sign, while in others it is a most insulting gesture. The same ambivalence can be seen in the 'v' sign. Like the sign of the phallus itself, the dual meaning, lucky and hostile, indicates that the gesture is an important and powerful one. What does it represent? The writers of the 1865 *Essay on the Worship of the Generative Powers* had no doubt that it was a symbol for actual sexual intercourse, the thumb representing the penis lodged in the vagina, and this interpretation is also favoured by a modern authority such as Desmond Morris. The sign is called *mano fica* in modern Italian, and this is usually taken to mean 'fig hand'; the Italian for 'fig', however, is *fico*, not *fica*: the latter is a slang term for the vulva. The similarity of the two words is hardly coincidental, since the fig is one of the better natural objects which provides a visual pun for the female parts. The hand gesture is surely intended to represent the female genitals themselves, and amulets such as 57 therefore depict both male and female, the latter being perhaps more unequivocally portrayed in this indirect way than by an attempt at realism. The possible ambiguity of the 'phallus and eye' illustrations is not present here, and the female sign must simply be reinforcing the apotropaic power of the amulet.

There are two further small and rather restricted groups of objects of the Roman Imperial period which seem to depict the female genitals in a fairly recognisable way. Lamps such as 58 have ornamental handles, often quite definitely modelled in the form of a leaf, and the type of handle shown has sometimes been interpreted as a stylised leaf. On appearance alone, it seems far more likely to be a careful, though simplified, study of the vulva. If so, the function of this vulvate handle, if any, must have been apotropaic, just as the many lamps with phallic decoration would have had this type of power. A purely decorative function cannot be entirely ruled out, however.

The other category is a very small one, a group of somewhat strange antefixes from York. Antefixes were the vertical roof-tiles which decorated the eaves of Roman (and Greek) buildings, and were often elaborated into highly decorative forms. It was very common indeed for these to have luck-bringing devices, as they were well placed to bring fortune and protection to the whole building which they

58 *below* Roman lamp-handle in vulvate form, with the same apotropaic function as the phallus. 1st century AD

59 *below right* Terracotta roof-ornament (antefix) from York, depicting a female head surrounded by a decorative frame which may be intended to represent a vulva. 2nd century AD

adorned. Provincial Roman antefixes are usually plainer than those from Italy, and are of triangular form, with quite simple decoration in relief. The best known examples from Britain are those which bear the name, number and symbol of a legion, and were made at the appropriate legionary pottery. The York examples are decorated in an extraordinary way (59). The central motif is a female head, and in this a long tradition is being followed, since female faces are commonly found on antefixes in the Mediterranean area centuries earlier. The York female heads are crudely executed and are surrounded by an elaborate border with a knob-like projection at the top. Visually, the effect is certainly reminiscent of a vulva, and it may well be intentional. The association with a female head may imply a connection with some Celtic female deity whose protective power was being invoked. It will be remembered that the phallus, too, is often associated with a head. Certainly in medieval times, the display of female genitals seems to have been used to confer protection on buildings; the most famous examples are the so-called 'shiela-na-gigs' found on Irish churches, but there are other displaying female figures in medieval European sculpture. This is particularly interesting, as there seems to be relatively little in the way of classical antecedents. It is virtually only in Roman Egypt that figurines of women actually displaying their genitals occur, and they are somewhat outside the main classical tradition. A mythological story, that of Baubo, is used to explain these Romano-Egyptian statuettes. The York vulvas, if that is what they are, may be references to Celtic goddesses of the kind which are known from later literary sources, able to appear in numerous transformations, including hideously hag-like ones with grossly exaggerated genitals.

From a careful consideration of the evidence, it seems clear that in classical antiquity images of the genitals, male or female, were not normally intended to have any purpose connected with sexual feelings as such. If we wish to understand them in their ancient context, it is a wholly inappropriate reaction to regard them as obscene, or even as sexual. There may, of course, have been those who, even in antiquity, regarded amulets of this kind as amusing or a little embarrassing, because they expressed the beliefs of a very primitive and unsophisticated level of religious thought: this is nevertheless a very different reaction from that of recent scholars who cannot conceive of images of this kind having any meaning other than a provocatively erotic one. Scholars have been intellectually aware of the importance of phallic symbolism for generations, but emotional responses have still caused the suppression of material of this nature, introducing a bias into the surviving evidence which it can ill afford.

It is particularly important to make a distinction between apotropaic amulets of the kind discussed in this chapter and the truly erotic representations which we shall consider later. They form a specific category, not quite in the purely religious area touched on in the previous chapter, but certainly separate from the scenes of lovemaking which have no religious *raison d'être*. The true extent of the use of such amulets in the Roman period has been obscured in the past by their exclusion from some collections, and by their treatment, generally, as 'erotica', a definition which belies their real function.

4 Dionysos and drama

In our earlier consideration of religion, we referred briefly to the god Dionysos, or Bacchus, as one of the many deities connected with fertility. Fuller discussion has been left for this chapter since the cult of Dionysos has very great importance for our theme as a whole. He is thought of principally as a wine-god, and though this is true up to a point – his orgiastic and ecstatic rites did make use of the consumption of wine – it is only part of the story. He was connected more with the fertility of plants than of animals, and the metaphor of death and rebirth which is typical of such gods, mirroring the new growth of vegetation each year, is one of the features which links the cult of Dionysos with other personal mystery religions, including Christianity. The power and importance of his worship in the ancient world depended, too, on the high degree of personal involvement felt by his worshippers: the Bacchic ecstasy was a form of oneness with the god, and to take full part in the rites one was possessed and set outside oneself. The real meaning of ecstasy turns on the concept of being 'beside oneself'. This condition is not unconnected with the requirements of acting, insofar as the actor must set aside his own personality and take on another. The Bacchic worshippers who took the parts of the mythical beings in the god's retinue were, in a sense, acting, and it is in the context of Bacchic worship that one of the great cultural contributions which antiquity made to later times grew up, namely the theatre of the Greeks.

Dionysos was a relative late-comer to the Greek pantheon, and it was believed by the ancients, probably correctly, that his worship originated in Thrace or further east. As with many other deities, there were numerous and contradictory myths concerning his origins, but the most popular, which eventually became the usual version, is that he was a son of Zeus, the highest god, and a mortal woman called Semele. The jealous Hera impelled Semele to ask her divine lover if she might see him as he was amongst the gods; this was an unwise move for a mortal, and Semele was, predictably, consumed by fire. Her unborn child, Dionysos, was rescued by his father Zeus, who enclosed him in his own thigh, whence he was born at the proper time. One of the later exploits of Dionysos was to bring about the immortality of his mother by rescuing her from the underworld, and establishing her, re-named Thyone, amongst the gods on Mount Olympus.

As a young god, Dionysos wandered far and wide over the sea to many countries, including India. Where he was well received, he rewarded men with the knowledge of the cultivation of the vine and the production of wine. Where he was not accorded the respect due to his divine rank, his revenge tended to be violent and merciless. A few examples must suffice. The Thracian king Lycurgus was one who rejected Dionysos, driving the god from his lands and imprisoning his followers. As a punishment, his country was afflicted with sterility and he himself with insanity, so that he imagined his own son to be a hated vine plant and hacked him to pieces. Eventually Lycurgus was trampled to death by wild horses and through this blood sacrifice fertility returned to the country. Another equally unfortunate and ill-advised king was Pentheus, ruler of Thebes. Like Lycurgus, he took exception to Dionysos and the nature of his worship, and was torn to pieces by his own mother, Agave, while she was a frenzied Maenad, one of the female followers of the god. This story is told in Euripides' tragic drama *The Bacchae*. Both these myths contain the element of human sacrifice, and it seems likely that an early phase of the cult may have included this element in reality,

60 *previous page* The theatre of Dionysos at Athens.

61 The Lycurgus cup; a late-Roman carved glass cup illustrating the legend of Lycurgus. 4th century AD

though it would have been reduced in time to animal sacrifice.

Another myth which illustrates Bacchus's indignation when the worship due to him was not forthcoming, and also mentions his seafaring activities, concerns a group of pirates who once seized him, in the hope that he was a rich prisoner worth robbing. Their attempts to bind him fast on their ship failed, and one member of the crew realised that they were dealing with a supernatural being. He tried to persuade his companions to desist, but failed. Dionysos changed all the pirates, with the exception of the one rather more percipient sailor, into dolphins, and caused vines to sprout from the mast of the ship. This tale is depicted in a black-figure cup painted by the artist Exekias, now in Munich. The arrival of Dionysos from the sea was celebrated in the various processions and feasts in

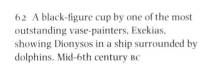

62 A black-figure cup by one of the most outstanding vase-painters, Exekias, showing Dionysos in a ship surrounded by dolphins. Mid-6th century BC

15 *opposite* A Roman marble relief of Hercules and a nymph.

Greece, where he was shown on a wheeled ship-cart.

Stories such as those of Lycurgus and Pentheus demonstrate very clearly the unrestrained and orgiastic nature of the cult; the Maenads were liable to tear limb from limb any creature, human or animal, which crossed their path. The combination of music, dancing and wine-drinking was (and still is) conducive to wild and uninhibited behaviour, and to the development of that state of ecstasy which, in appropriate circumstances, could be interpreted as possession by the

17 Part of a Dionysiac scene decorating a magnificent bronze crater found at Dherveni, Macedonia. Late 4th century BC

16 *left* Detail from the great silver dish in the Mildenhall (Suffolk) Treasure, showing the god Pan dancing, as part of the Bacchic thiasos. 4th century AD

18 *right* A marble herm of Hermes from Siphnos. *c.* 520 BC

19 The violent death of Pentheus,
illustrated in a painting from the House of
the Vettii at Pompeii. 1st century AD

63 *above* Dionysos, accompanied by satyrs and maenads, on a black-figure vase by the Euphiletos Painter. 530–500 BC

64 *below* Red-figure amphora by the Nikon Painter, with a herm of Dionysos and an altar. 475–450 BC

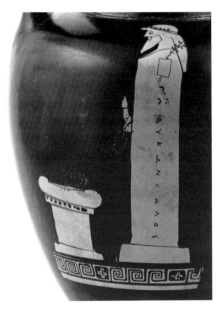

god himself. The cult of Bacchus involved a considerable supporting cast of human and mythical beings, the *thiasos*. We shall consider these participants in due course, since they are represented, often indulging in riotous and licentious behaviour, on Greek painted pottery and appear in other contexts up to the late Roman period.

Representations of Dionysos himself in early vase-paintings scarcely convey the impression of a wild and orgiastic fertility deity. Even though his influence over the vine and other growing things clearly mark him as a fertility god, he is not himself depicted as ithyphallic, except very occasionally in the form of a herm (64). On black-figure pottery (63) he is shown as a dignified, bearded god wearing a long robe and crowned with vine leaves, retaining a solemn and restrained bearing however wild the cavortings of the followers who surround him. As time went on, this image of Dionysos changed somewhat, and in Hellenistic and Roman times he had become a youthful beardless god, sometimes a little effeminate in bearing and more involved in the rites of his own worship, to the extent on occasion of being seen in a drunken state. The Bacchus of the Mildenhall dish (30) is a representation of the fourth century AD, and shows this younger and more 'human' version of the god, though in this instance he remains a strikingly dignified figure.

The members of the Bacchic entourage, the thiasos, encompassed a wide range of beings. The human female devotees were called Maenads, Bacchantes or Lenae. In their ecstatic intoxication they are depicted in art dancing in an abandoned manner, their heads thrown back and their hair disordered, sometimes waving aloft the torn portions of animals which they have dismembered in their frenzy. Musical instruments are often shown – tambourines, castanets, flutes. Another frequent attribute is the *thyrsos*, a staff topped with a large pine-cone, itself a symbol of fruitfulness. The thyrsos can be used by Maenads to fend off the amorous advances of the satyrs and sileni who form one of the main non-human elements in the god's retinue.

To distinguish between sileni and satyrs is a hopeless task: it is obvious that, though the origins of these two types of half-human beings were certainly diverse, during antiquity confusion grew up between them, and iconographic changes and development make it simpler to regard them as more or less the same. They are also confused with the god Pan, often in his plural form, and by late antiquity, probably also with Faunus, another plural god. Satyrs seem at first to have had goat-like characteristics, like the god Pan, while the sileni had the ears, tails and sometimes the hoofs, of horses. Both species were rural spirits who, being half-animal, were able to behave in ways which would not have been acceptable for humans. In effect, they embody the animal side of human nature, seen as a separate quality. Some representations have almost monkey-like faces, and until well into the Roman period, satyrs are often shown with coarse snub noses and animal ears. They were lustful beings, constantly chasing nymphs, mortal women and even goddesses, their intentions obvious from their sexually aroused state. Their genitals are usually represented as altogether larger than those of humans. Vase-paintings commonly depict them as failing to achieve their sexual ends, being successfully fought off by indignant females of various human, divine and other species. They tend to succeed best with quadrupeds such as deer and goats, to whom they are, of course, closely related – compare the famous

65 *below* A Roman marble sarcophagus carved with scenes of Bacchic revelry; the god himself is seen in the centre, drunk and supported by satyrs. Second half of the 2nd century AD

66 *opposite* Black-figure vase (Tyrrhenian amphora) with a Dionysiac scene or komos. Second quarter of the 6th century BC

67 A red-figure cup by Epiktetos, decorated with a satyr pursuing a maenad. Last quarter of the 6th century BC

Herculaneum Pan (*I*). This lack of sexual success is a feature of the entertaining aspect of satyrs; though they could, surely, be frightening on occasion, they are seen mainly as amusingly incompetent, idle and greedy. Their presence is central to the Bacchic thiasos and to the development of drama, for the very earliest form of dramatic performance in the service of Dionysos, the satyr-plays, featured human actors dressed as satyrs or sileni.

By the time of the early Roman Empire, though the type of the satyr continued in the form of Pans or Fauns, the satyrs themselves had become somewhat tamer, handsome young men retaining only a small goat tail and perhaps a discreet pair of horns or pointed ears as a reminder of animal ancestry. Such satyrs are still present in fourth-century art, for example, on the Mildenhall dish again, or the gold buckle from the Thetford treasure (68). Pan himself is repeatedly shown as part of the Bacchic entourage, as is Silenos, the archetypal silen. Silenos, also called Papposilenos, had been the teacher of the young Dionysos, and in spite of his rumbustious behaviour possessed great wisdom and soothsaying powers; Faunus, it will be remembered, was also a god with the powers of a seer. Silenos frequently appears as a portly and inebriated figure, supported by helpful satyrs, or balancing precariously on the back of a donkey, an animal which is often present in the Bacchic circle. Other creatures which appear in art among Dionysiac scenes include the goat, naturally, deer, snakes and, above all, the panther, which is the close companion of the god himself. Sometimes a tiger appears, a reference to the god's sojourn in India.

Another hybrid animal-human species which sometimes takes part in Bacchic activity is the centaur. Very early illustrations of these combinations of horse and man provide them with a totally human forepart and the body and hindquarters

of a horse, but the classic type has a complete equine body, with the torso of a man rising from the horse's shoulders. Though myths of centaurs stress their wild and untrustworthy behaviour, there is, as with Silenos, an element of wisdom and learning. The centaur Chiron was the teacher of many heroes, including Achilles.

In addition to these beings, various nymphs and others formed part of Bacchus's entourage, and minor gods such as Priapus may on occasion be involved. The group as a whole exemplifies nature both in its rougher and its more graceful manifestations, all taking part in a celebration of life and growth. The survival of Bacchic worship into late-Roman times has already been mentioned, and in the period when Christianity had become the official and accepted religion it was one of the more important forms of paganism still practised; it did, after all, offer the kind of personal involvement which was lacking in the main Graeco-Roman pantheon. The Roman Bacchanalia were festivals of some importance, but it is the Greek festivals of Dionysos which most concern us here, particularly in the form in which they were celebrated in Attica, since it was in the context of these religious rituals that the Greek drama grew up.

Four major Attic festivals of Dionysos are known: the rural, or lesser Dionysia, celebrated in December; the Lenaea, in January; the Anthesteria in February; and the most important of all, the City or great Dionysia, which took place for a whole week in the month Elaphebolion, March to early April. For this latter festival, held as it was in the spring, there were generally many visitors from outside Athens itself; the earlier feasts had a more local character, as the weather was less suitable for travellers to make their way to Athens, especially by sea.

The name of the Lenaea is connected with one of the names for Maenads, Lenae. Not a great deal is known of the nature of the festival, but dramatic performances certainly took place, and it is known that some of the plays by the greatest writer of Greek comedy, Aristophanes, were first performed at the Lenaea. The Anthesteria was a celebration of the vintage, at which the new wine was tasted. One of the days of the feast was called *choes* – 'jugs', from the wine-jugs that were used. Miniature versions of these jugs were given to children, and examples of these have survived, decorated very often with scenes of children playing.

The rural Dionysia were more directly concerned in the development of the drama as part of the worship of Dionysos. Taking place as they did in the winter, the hope of fertility for the coming year was a part of their purpose, and the type of dance which was performed, the *komos*, had a markedly phallic character. Performers were dressed as satyrs, and an outsize model phallus was borne aloft by *phallopheroi* (meaning 'phallus-bearers') – while songs and revels took place. The dressing-up as satyrs is part of the basis for the more organised satyr-play, which is in turn the ultimate source of the true drama, tragedy as well as comedy. The dressing-up was not purely frivolous, but was also a religious experience, transforming the participants into part of the god's thiasos. Actual plays were eventually performed at the rural Dionysia, but these remained an altogether more rustic festival than the great Dionysia as held at Athens. Music and dancing, as well as drinking, were essential features of the worship of Bacchus, and the hymns which were sung or chanted by choruses at these feasts had a special name, the *dithyramb*. Dithyrambs were performed competitively at the City Dionysia, somewhat in the manner, perhaps, of the proceedings at an eisteddfod.

As we have seen, the City Dionysia took place in Athens in the spring, and was attended by many visitors from other areas of Greece. The event was on a scale which required elaborate bureaucratic organisation, lasting a week and involving as many as a thousand active participants, not to mention the spectators: the theatre of Dionysos in Athens probably accommodated an audience of about 14,000. Though the precise form of the celebrations varied over the years, and the length of the festival had to be curtailed on occasion owing to war, certain features were constant. There were processions at the beginning which included a figure of the god borne aloft on a ship-cart, the *carrum navale*. This later Latin name may be connected with the origin of the word 'carnival' as well as with the carnival 'float' itself. After the processions and the appropriate religious observances (e.g. sacrifices) the dithyramb competitions took place, performed by choruses of fifty each from the ten tribes. The dramatic competitions came next, first the comedies and then three tetralogies, sets of three tragedies, each followed by a satyr-play. All this was financed by patrons called *choregoi*, 'chorus-leaders': they were wealthy citizens selected for this expensive and compulsory honour by the archon, the chief magistrate for the year.

Both plays and dithyrambs were adjudicated, and prizes were awarded to the victorious choruses and poets; the poets' prizes were a bull for the first place, an amphora of wine for the second, and a goat for the third, all clearly connected with the worship of Dionysos which was the *raison d'être* for the whole event. Because the relatively few surviving plays have had such an enormous influence on the course and development of European literature, it can be difficult to remember that the original reason for this combination of literary festival and mass entertainment was in fact religious. The religious element was already diminished by the Roman period, and the drama was increasingly seen as one of many forms of entertainment.

It is not necessary for our purpose to consider in detail the architecture of Greek and Roman theatres and the differences between the Greek and the Roman, but the general form has to be known before one can fully understand the nature of the performances which took place in them. The overall appearance of an ancient theatre is probably fairly familiar to most people, if only because many of these impressive sites still survive, some in sufficiently good condition to be used for dramatic performances still. The rising tiers of seats were, where possible, set into a hillside to minimise the amount of building. The spectators, sitting on cushions on their stone seats, looked down from the open-air auditorium on to a stage with an open area, the orchestra ('dancing-place') in front of it. The details of the *skene*, the stage, varied, and though they are not precisely known, scholars of the subject are able to infer a good deal from the plays themselves and from some illustrations in vase-paintings and, later, from Roman wall-paintings in buildings. Some surviving Roman theatres, such as those at Orange and at Sabratha (Libya) still have clear traces of an elaborate multi-storied stage building. Scenery was used, and there were certain forms of machinery for special effects – an arrangement which could change the scene, like a revolving stage, and a hoist which could bring characters on in mid-air, useful for moments of divine intervention in the action.

In spite of this, it must not be thought that realism was the quality striven for in Greek drama. On the contrary, the structure of Greek plays was very formalised, showing clear evidence of their ritualistic origins. Only three or, at most, four actors were permitted. This could mean that each actor might play several roles, perhaps of very different kinds. The chorus (whose leader also had a speaking part, though he was not counted as one of the actors) played a major part. As well as being involved in the action, the chorus kept the audience informed of events which took place off-stage, and performed songs and dances relevant to the play. This arrangement in itself gives a feeling of ritual to the proceedings, as anyone can confirm who has seen a Greek drama performed with reasonable faithfulness in modern times. It is, however, no more extraordinary than the structure of a modern opera or musical comedy, though to us it seems a strange form for tragedy.

The actors (there were, of course, no actresses) wore garments which helped to make them clearly visible to the large audience, many of whom were a considerable distance away from the stage: padded robes, built-up boots and masks, the latter clearly indicating the nature of the drama, comedy or tragedy, and the type of character portrayed. There were stock masks, but individual ones were also sometimes used in comedy, specially made to resemble a public figure known to the audience and thus underline a satiric point of the dramatist's. The comic and tragic masks remain a universally understood symbol of drama two-and-a-half millennia after they were introduced. The satyr players were likewise masked to resemble the beings they portrayed, with snub noses and long beards: they also wore special loin-cloths designed to complete the satyr image, furry or spotted like an animal's pelt, and equipped with the essential attributes of a tail

69 Red-figure cup by Makron. The figure is of a satyr-player rather than a 'real' satyr, wearing a loin-cloth incorporating a phallus and tail. 500–475 BC

behind and an artificial phallus made of leather in front. Examples of these satyr players, easily distinguishable from 'real' satyrs in mythological scenes, can be found on some vase-paintings (69).

In its earlier phases of development, the actors taking male parts in comedy also wore artificial genitals of noteworthy proportions, together with a bulbously padded body clothed in a very short tunic, and the grotesquely grinning mask. The name 'comedy' is derived from the komos, the dance of the Bacchic revellers, and the plays take over much from their slapstick improvisations and phallic songs. Many of the passing comments and allusions in surviving plays belonging

70 A mosaic showing actors in a satyr-play. From the House of the Tragic Poet at Pompeii.

to the period of Old Comedy are fully comprehensible only if the impropriety of the characters' clothing and their exaggerated sexual attributes are borne in mind. Plays of this genre were taken via the Greek colonies to Italy, and though they eventually developed in different ways from the comedy of Greece, the costumes were similar. The Italian popular comedy is often illustrated on South Italian painted pottery.

The outstanding poet of Old Comedy was Aristophanes, eleven of whose plays, from a total of perhaps forty, have survived. He lived from about 450 BC to about 385, a period which was marked by the long-drawn-out Peloponnesian War, in which there was constant strife between Athens and the other Greek states. This fact makes some characteristics of Old Comedy all the more remarkable. The comic plays of this period did not consist solely of knockabout fun and coarse jokes, though they certainly contained these elements in profusion: there was parody, for example, of tragedies and, above all, there was a very strong element of satire. Comedy could, in fact, be made to convey messages every bit as serious as those of tragedy, though packaged in a lighthearted manner. Satire which involves outspoken criticism of the government and the conduct of a war while that war is actually in progress sounds a very dangerous thing, and it is a measure of Athenian democracy in the fifth century BC that such satire was acceptable.

Probably the best known of Aristophanes' plays is his *Lysistrata*, first performed at the Lenaea in 411 BC, at a time of tense military impasse between Athens and Sparta. While the sexual jokes and references in other comedies can to some extent be bowdlerised, leaving the plot more or less intact, *Lysistrata* is a prude's nightmare, as the whole plot is a sexual joke. Aristophanes imagined a situation in which the women of Greece, Spartans as well as Athenians, in their exasperation at the apparently endless war, decided to take matters into their own hands: under the leadership of the enterprising and determined Lysistrata, they deny their menfolk any sexual access until they conclude a peace treaty. The theme is full of opportunities for coarse jokes and for slapstick, with two choruses of old men and old women respectively taking a lively part in the action. There are repeated references to the pathetically frustrated condition of the men, which would have been graphically illustrated by the nature of the costume. Bawdy is being used here on at least three levels, though the first was probably too basic to the form to have been considered consciously by the poet: in the first place, the phallic element in comedy was part of the religious rite to which the whole festival was dedicated, Dionysos being a fertility deity. This was exemplified in the form of the costumes, derived from the komasts and satyrs. Secondly, the sexual element was funny, and was meant to be enjoyed as pure humour; thirdly, the whole was intended to illustrate a serious point, and in the circumstances a politically delicate one – *Lysistrata* criticises warfare in general, and the conduct of the current war in particular.

Comedy continued to change and develop, and in the succeeding century the outstanding poet of the phase known as New Comedy was Menander (*c.* 343 – *c.* 292 BC). The themes become less concerned with political satire and more with daily life, certain stock characters being used repeatedly. The openly indecent element also declines, and the costumes of the Old Comedy survive only to a minor extent in the garb of certain characters such as slaves and rustics. Much later, in the Roman Empire, there were certainly forms of entertainment which were blatantly sexual, but they were not combined with plays of genuine literary merit. This combination, of outrageous bawdy and poetic genius, can only flower now and then, and Athens in the fifth century BC was one of those rare occasions. There are echoes of the comedy, perhaps, even on provincial Roman pottery in the first and second centuries AD. In 17 we see a figure-type which occurs on decorated samian ware at that period and which seems to depict not so much a satyr as someone dressed as a satyr, for the exaggerated phallus can hardly be a natural one.

The Greek comedy and the related forms of drama in Italy can be seen to have contained throughout a very powerful element of bawdy, which was not merely acceptable to the audiences and the authorities, but essential. The analogy with Shakespearean drama is a striking one. From the plays and the illustrations on pottery and in terracottas one can gain some idea of what the audiences found funny, and perhaps extend this knowledge to other objects which we suspect may have been intended to amuse. It is not always easy to enter into the humour of other cultures, even contemporary ones, so it could well be that some of the objects which I shall go on to discuss, in the belief that they were visual sexual jokes, may have had some hidden and more weighty purpose. It is certain that some of them had, like the comedy itself, a dual purpose, and were, for instance, articles of use as well as amusement.

In our discussion of apotropaic objects and deities such as Priapus in previous chapters, we have seen that phallic representations were considered amusing as well as lucky, and of course the attitude shown in Old Comedy fully confirms this. We can return first to the satyrs themselves, and the numerous representations of their often ill-fated sexual activities which appear on black-figure and red-figure vases.

There is more than one representation of a satyr using his erect organ as a convenient hook on which to hang some article – in one case the container for the pipes which he is playing. The revelling satyrs on the splendid wine-cooler (3) include one in their number who has an even more impressive trick: he is balancing a wine-cup on the tip of his phallus. The numerous illustrations which show satyrs being repulsed by Maenads and others, such as 20, were also undoubtedly considered entertaining. The tendency of satyrs to try anything, sexually speaking, is nicely exemplified on the cup in 71, where one member of the roistering band is making a hopeful, and perhaps slightly doubtful, approach to one of the two distinctly remote-looking sphinxes which flank the scene. It seems likely that this satyr will have to resort ultimately to the same form of gratification as his colleague in 72, which shows two sides of the same black-figure vessel. The theme of masturbation does not appear to be very common, though there are quite a few vase-paintings depicting women wielding very large dildoes: since this is not a very realistic concept of female masturbation, it seems likely that they are hetairai laying on a particular type of entertainment for their clients. Whether the theme was considered funny is not entirely clear, though most satyr activities can be interpreted in this way. The painting in 73 is a somewhat different case, however, as the figures are definitely men rather than satyrs.

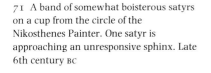

71 A band of somewhat boisterous satyrs on a cup from the circle of the Nikosthenes Painter. One satyr is approaching an unresponsive sphinx. Late 6th century BC

72 Two sides of a black-figure vase decorated with a masturbating satyr. 6th century BC

73 The theme of masturbation on a black-figure cup by the Amasis Painter. 530–520 BC

Notwithstanding the powerfully apotropaic function of the phallus alone, it seems likely that many of the objects which were intended as charms may also have been considered amusing, such as the animal-phallus tintinnabula. At the same time, phallic themes were considered appropriate in a funerary context: the oil-flask (74) is a type not infrequently found in graves, yet it seems likely that the conceit of making a whole pottery vessel in the form of a set of male genitals can hardly have been a wholly solemn one. Likewise, the cup with genitalia instead of a pedestal base (76) must have raised a laugh with the guests at any dinner-party where it was used, but the eye motif is also present in the decoration, so that the apotropaic idea is not far away. The dividing line between apotropaic function and humour is far from clear.

Turning from Greece to Rome, there are naturally many possible and definite examples of sexual humour in the wealth of material from Pompeii. The famous and very beautiful bronze tripod supported by three markedly ithyphallic young satyrs may be an example. Also well known are several terracotta bowls in a form very reminiscent of a comic mask with a huge, gaping mouth (75). Within the bowls are phalluses, sometimes winged, modelled in the round. The precise use of these bowls is uncertain, but one plausible suggestion is that they are bird-bowls. The similarity of these to masks is a reminder that there are many grotesque representations in Roman times, as in Greek, which are possibly or certainly connected with the theatre, and which are often combined with phallic motifs – grotesque heads in terracotta, for example, in which a wart-like feature on the forehead is developed into a phallus form, or representations of phallus-nosed beings (77).

The theme of the personified phallus has already been discussed, but one example illustrated here seems to go beyond an apotropaic interpretation (78). It is a provincial Roman product, a colour-coated pottery beaker probably made in the Peterborough area. Other vessels of this type sometimes have decoration of several phalluses surrounding them and they can probably simply be regarded

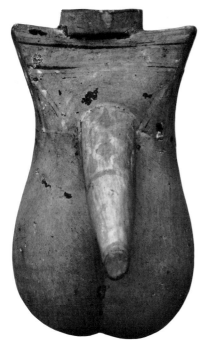

74 *above* Corinthian pottery oil-flask in phallic form. Second quarter of the 6th century BC

75 *right* Terracotta bowl from Pompeii: the vessel is in the form of a mask, and contains phalluses modelled in relief and in the round. 1st century AD

76 *below* A black-figure eye-cup with a phallic base in place of the normal pedestal foot. There is probably a combination here of good-luck symbol and humour. Second half of the 6th century BC

as good-luck charms, but comparison of this with another product of the same industry suggests that it has at least an element of parody about it. The technique of decoration is called *barbotine*, and consists of piping the decoration freehand on to the pot using a thick slip of clay, very much in the manner of decorating a cake with piped sugar icing. The technique is a formidably difficult one, and the degree of skill in its execution shown by the potters of Roman Britain and Gaul is impressive. The scenes most commonly depicted are hunting scenes with animals – hounds chasing deer, and so on. Human figures are more difficult to represent, and occur less often. Illustration 79 is a pot of this type with a circus scene on it

78 above Romano-British pottery beaker from Saffron Walden, Essex. The decoration is a phallic parody of a chariot-racing scene like that on the similar pot from Colchester (*79, right*), decorated with a chariot-racing scene. Both date from the third to the fourth century AD

77 below An elaborate apotropaic wall-carving with a phallus-nosed centaur, from Leptis Magna, Libya. Roman.

80 Two views of a Romano-British beaker
found at Horsey Toll, Cambridgeshire, and
made near Peterborough. The decoration
is probably intended to be entertaining as
well as erotic. 3rd century AD

of four racing chariots; even the characteristic costume of the charioteers is carefully shown. The chariots drawn by phalluses on the other beaker are obviously a direct parody of this, and the charioteer has become a naked female figure. The whole thing can be nothing other than an elaborate visual joke.

One assumes that the same is true of yet another Romano-British pot of the same type (80). The scene here is a very sexually outspoken one, and at first sight should perhaps belong in a later chapter amongst the strictly erotic representations. It seems to me, however, that the gross exaggeration of the scene, the disembodied phallus clasped by the female character, and the fact that the male protagonist is, as it were, anticipating the point of the encounter, all suggests that the picture is not to be taken seriously, but is simply supposed to cause merriment in the observer. It is hard to say how common such vessels were, since it is only in fairly recent years that a find of this kind would be likely to become generally known at all, but there cannot have been a great number, if only because a product like this would have taken up a good deal of the potter's time, and would therefore probably have been relatively expensive.

There may be many more examples of sexual depictions which would have been enjoyed as entertainment by the Greeks and Romans, but it is difficult for us to be sure of identifying them correctly. It is also hard to imagine quite the nature of their reaction as opposed to our own, because it seems likely that there is a different quality to sexual humour in an atmosphere where sex can have the very serious and religious connotations which we have already considered. Amongst other things, this state of affairs gives rise to a degree of familiarity with sexually explicit images which is quite foreign to our culture.

In this and the two preceding chapters we have considered various types of sexual images connected with religious ritual, with the drama which developed out of one particular religious cult, or which were for good luck or light entertainment. In the past such images have been classed as obscene and even today are still regarded in some circles as improper. The question of what constitutes obscenity is difficult to answer, and the scope of this book does not allow for discussion of its legal definition; the subject could occupy many volumes – and has done – without coming to a satisfactory conclusion. Most modern definitions, however, do require some intent to arouse sexual feeling, though obviously modern definitions do not have to contend with the problem of sexual arousal as a religious act.

If we regard all representations of sexual acts and organs for any purpose whatsoever as improper and indecent, then certainly some of the objects so far discussed would fall into such a category. If, on the other hand, we feel that there should be some distinction made between a religious ritual, a medical diagram, and an image intended to inflame sexual appetite for its own sake, then nothing so far discussed falls into that last category. That some of the representations, and indeed, the religious rituals themselves, may have given rise to sexual activity is not the point: none of the images we have looked at was primarily intended to arouse sexual excitement for its own sake in the beholder (though, perhaps, with the type of decoration mentioned immediately above, we are coming very near to this). It is our problem, rather than that of our ancestors in classical times, that we may find it difficult to detect any distinction of purpose between a good-luck pendant in the form of a stylised male organ, or a religious image, and a picture of a couple making love.

20 opposite A red-figure cup by Makron, showing a maenad defending herself with her thyrsos against an importunate satyr. *c.*480 BC

21 *left* A Roman marble relief of Leda and the Swan. This type of image, with an overwhelmingly large and powerful swan, stresses the fact that the animal is in fact Zeus in one of his many manifestations.

22 *below* A marble relief showing part of a Dionysiac procession. Roman.

23 Detail of a Roman marble
sarcophagus, with a female Pan and a
Pan-headed herm. Second half of the 2nd
century AD

24 A painting, part of a complete series, from the Villa of the Mysteries at Pompeii, showing flagellation as a religious rite. 1st century BC

5
Men and beasts

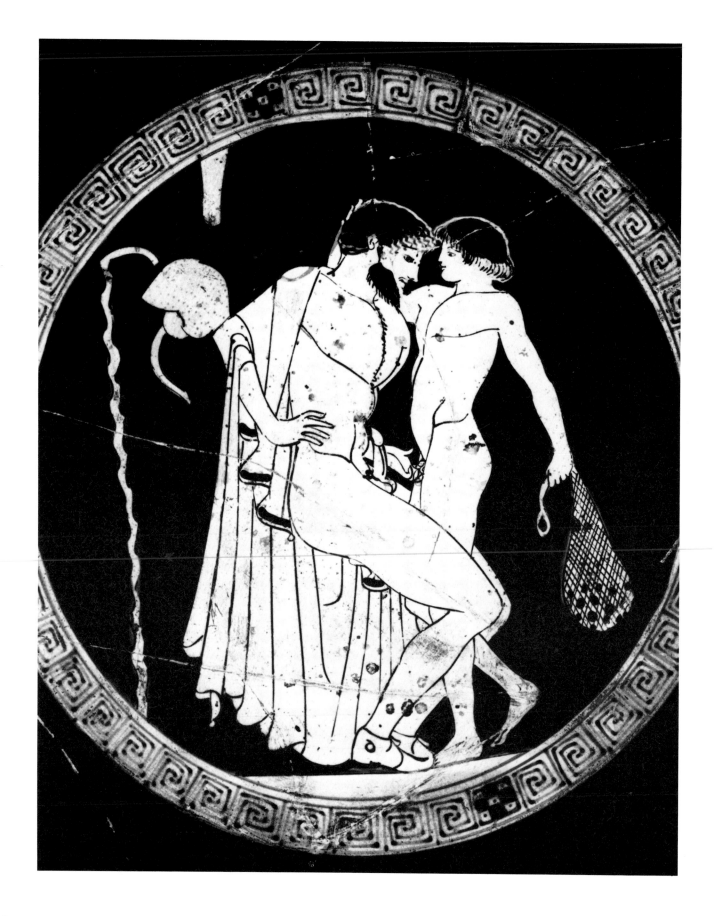

We have seen that a great many representations of sexual subjects in Greek and Roman art were intended primarily to serve religious or, at the very least, superstitious purposes, and were not meant to be sexually arousing as such. There is another category of material which can, in contrast, be defined as truly erotic. Many of the images of sexual activity are undoubtedly intended for titillation, and are therefore erotic in the full sense of the word. I am regarding scenes of courtship and actual copulation, when neither in an obviously religious framework, nor obviously humorous (as would be the case, for instance, in scenes involving satyrs) as falling into the category of real eroticism. Naturally, not everyone will agree in detail with particular examples; there may be scenes which I shall include in this chapter or the next which some would say belong under religion or humour, as well as some in other chapters which will be thought to be purely erotic. The test which I am trying to apply is not so much whether the scene may be sexually exciting – the definition of this is extremely personal – but whether some non-erotic element is of major importance in the image. In the next chapter, I shall deal with illustrations of heterosexual love making, but first we shall consider minority sexual interests and practices. In both cases, there will be occasional religious connotations, since deities and mythological beings were supposed to engage in a variety of sexual activities, and these are often illustrated.

Our main category in this chapter of 'minority' sex is homosexuality. It is well

81 *left* A scene of a man titillating a young boy, from a red-figure cup by the Brygos Painter. 500–475 BC

82 *below* A red-figure cup by Peithinos, showing men and youths courting. Late 6th century BC

known that this orientation was acceptable in ancient Greek society in a way which has certainly not been the case in most Christian communities, but its acceptability was far from simple and uncomplicated, and the way in which it is illustrated in Greek vase-paintings at least partially bears this out. The subject has been dealt with at length, using both literary and artistic evidence, in K.J. Dover's *Greek Homosexuality*, yet many unanswered questions remain. The type of relationship described by Professor Dover, and illustrated on black-figure and red-figure Attic pottery, is strictly between an adult male and a youth, not between men (or youths) of similar age. This type of homosexual relationship was fully accepted; indeed, it was apparently expected in some circumstances. It seems to have been considered perfectly normal for adult men to be deeply affected by the physical beauty of boys and adolescents, but the relationship between the man-and-youth couples which developed from this was very formalised, and there were rituals to observe. The literature and vase-paintings bear out the convention that the older lover (Dover uses the Greek words, *erastes* for the lover, *eromenos* for the youthful beloved) desired, and hoped to achieve, a sexual relationship, but the *eromenos* merely tolerated this, without deriving any direct physical or emotional satisfaction from it. The older man was able to confer various benefits on his young protégé – gifts, perhaps some social status, education in various fields: very much the kind of thing a father can give his son, or a teacher his pupil. The price the boy paid was the sexual attachment. The vase-paintings depict the youths submitting with a stoical and distant expression, and with a total lack of physical reaction, to the lovemaking of their older friends (83).

While accepting that in the peculiar circumstances of Athenian society at this period (the sixth to fourth centuries BC) young men may have been glad of the affection and guidance of adults of their own sex, because there was a lack of a warm family environment, and because the intelligence and potential social role of women was grossly underestimated, and while noting, too, that various forms of patronage were normal and widespread in the ancient world, it seems all the more curious that, having accepted the affection and closeness of an older man, a youth could submit to actual sexual love without responding in kind. Most adolescent males are rather easily sexually aroused, and if the young *eromenos* felt a genuine affection for his lover, it seems somewhat unlikely that he could remain sexually unmoved and indifferent in his embrace. One wonders whether the vase-paintings here are depicting an ideal form of behaviour, a kind of approved etiquette for homosexual relations, rather than the normal state of affairs.

The paintings often show men presenting gifts in the courtship of their sometimes reluctant youths: animals such as cockerels and hares seem to have been especially favoured. In one of the scenes on the vase in 27, one of the gifts is the unwieldly one of a cockerel (one of the boys in this group does apparently show some degree of sexual response, but this is unusual). The initial approaches recorded generally consist of the man touching the face and genitals of the youth, while the latter often tries to keep him at arm's length, displaying perhaps a becoming and 'maidenly' modesty. If consummation is achieved, it is normally intercourse in a standing position, the man's penis between the youth's thighs. Anal intercourse is not very commonly shown, either in homosexual or heterosexual activities: I do not agree with Dover's interpretation of the many vase-paintings featuring male-female coitus from behind, in which he claims anal penetration is intended, but we shall discuss this more fully in the next chapter.

83 Black-figure vase with a homosexual courting scene. Mid-6th century BC

It is hardly surprising that in a society in which women were so underrated and the qualities of the male athlete and warrior so prized, that this form of homosexual behaviour should be tolerated. There seems to be little indication, however, of the attitude towards homosexual love between adults. The vase paintings show far more sexual activity between men and women than between men and youths, and apparently none between adult males. It was important for the Greek state that men should marry and engender children, so that from this point of view alone adult homosexual couples would have been failing in their duty as citizens. Nevertheless, the complete understanding of the physical attraction of male to male must surely have made tolerance of this orientation far greater than it has been in more recent societies. Though perhaps disapproved of in some circumstances, it would have been impossible for male homosexuality to have been regarded with the hysterical and senseless disgust and loathing which some Christians have accorded it.

Evidence of homosexuality in Roman art is relatively slight. Out of the scores of figure-types from pottery lamps which depict sexual scenes, there seems to be only one with a homosexual theme, and that is probably satirical. In other forms of decorated pottery, Arretine ware produces one or two homosexual scenes of the delicacy and elegance usual in the best period of this ware; similar examples exist in silver. Erotic scenes on Arretine normally show heterosexual couples at *symposia* (parties of a kind we shall discuss further on), and the homosexual groups are precisely parallel to the more usual heterosexual ones. Both the art of the Augustan period, when Arretine was made, and the concept of the symposium were consciously hellenising, so this, too, may be a factor in the treatment of homosexual themes. There is one figure-type recorded on South Gaulish samian ware of the late first century AD which appears to show anal intercourse between males, but it is excessively rare. Whatever the attitude to homosexuality, it was not a focus of interest to the decorators of pottery, or presumably the buyers, in the way that heterosexual behaviour was. The subject is mentioned as a matter of course in some writings, for example Suetonius's lives of the Caesars, or Petronius's *Satyricon*. Hadrian, an emperor who had a deep admiration for all things Greek, was able openly to mourn the death of his beautiful young friend Antinous, name cities after him, and set up a cult in his honour: it is true that the behaviour of an emperor could be criticised only with caution, and at some risk, but even so the impression that comes over is that a homosexual or bi-sexual orientation was not a cause for any great excitement, that it was accepted as a taste which could be indulged, like any other, in a restrained way or a licentious one according to character. If this was the case, it demonstrates one area at least in which the Romans were notably more civilised than ourselves.

Female homosexuality seems largely to be ignored in both Greek and Roman representations. It is true that a number of vase-paintings depict women brandishing *olisboi* (dildoes), but this is likely to have been for the entertainment of males: there is no need for such equipment between female lovers, though most men would like to think there is. The life of respectable women in Greece must have been conducive at the very least to strong emotional attachments between women, and it seems fair to assume that actual lesbianism may have been not uncommon. The fact that it is not mentioned in such contexts as Aristophanes' *Lysistrata* is irrelevant, since the heterosexuality, and consequently the frustration of the women as well as the men, is part of his dramatic purpose. The very term 'lesbian' is of course derived from the island of Lesbos, the home of the poet Sappho, who is thought of as the archetype of the homosexual woman. Sappho, who lived in the early sixth century BC, was highly regarded as a poet in her own time, and may have stood in a relationship to certain chosen and gifted young women similar to that of Socrates to his young men – a mentor and inspiration. The poetry which survives is far too fragmentary for the full story to be known, though it certainly includes some of the most telling descriptions of physical passion, and it is fair to say that those in later periods, during which more of her work was still extant than today, regarded her as homosexual.

In Rome there was again relatively little interest in female love-life when not angled towards men, and the general conclusion which presents itself is that the female sub-culture was simply not of sufficient interest to the predominantly male artists and writers for them to trouble to chronicle it. It is interesting that some other periods, in particular the nineteenth century, though just as male-orientated, found the thought of sexual activity between women intriguing and stimulating where the Greeks and Romans evidently found it boring. Perhaps this is due to the altogether more prurient attitude towards sex in recent times, but it is a curious contrast. This is not to say that descriptions of lesbian lovemaking in Victorian pornography are either sensitive or realistic; they are not. Whatever the reasons, images of female homosexual behaviour appear to be virtually absent from Greek and Roman art. Dover illustrates a vase-painting which depicts one

84 Replica of a Roman silver cup with a homosexual scene. Similar designs are known on Arretine pottery of the same period, the late first century BC and early first AD.

woman touching another in the genital region, and considers that it could indicate a sexual relationship between two hetairai, but though it certainly shows a degree of intimacy, it does not seem to have the air of a love-scene.

Before moving on to the other main 'minority' sexual theme which is illustrated by openly erotic illustrations, there are one or two areas of mythology which can, perhaps, best be treated here. One of these concerns the mythical being called Hermaphrodite, who is quite frequently represented in the visual arts, especially in the Hellenistic period. The name is a combination of Hermes and Aphrodite, but the history of the being, who can scarcely be called a deity, is obscure. One myth has it that he was originally a handsome youth who fell in love with a nymph, and became so inextricably unified with her as to form a single being of dual sex. This is a mythological expression of an urge familiar enough to lovers.

Hermaphrodite is represented in art as a figure with a feminine face, well developed breasts and hips, and male genitalia. The concept which is embodied here could be mystical in part, arising from the belief that the striving of the two sexes towards each other reflects an original creation in which both sexes were incorporated in each individual; more practically, it illustrates the actual existence in each person of male and female characteristics. Then again, the reasons for depicting such a creature could be more frivolous, and in some Roman

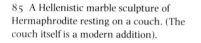

85 A Hellenistic marble sculpture of Hermaphrodite resting on a couch. (The couch itself is a modern addition).

art there are many light-hearted scenes in which an eager satyr or Pan uncovers what he takes to be a luscious sleeping nymph, only to start back nonplussed at the unexpected sight of the sleeper's penis. In yet other cases satyrs are shown enjoying very satisfactory sexual relationships with Hermaphrodite. The being does represent an ideal for certain male homosexuals, those who admire the general lines of the female body, but are distressed by the female genitals. Statuettes (86), paintings, and some fine-quality sculpture (85) exist devoted to the subject of this intersexed being, and there is little doubt that in the Hellenistic and early Roman periods at least, he was seen as an erotic figure, combining the physical beauties and attractions of both sexes. Classical art excelled in depicting monsters with elegance and conviction, and this is a particularly refined example of the genre.

Another somewhat limited area of mythological eroticism concerns a rare, but not unique, type which shows a sleeping man ravished by a Siren, a mythical creature with a woman's body but the wings and legs of a bird. The marble relief which is illustrated (87) is not the only example known, since the scene also occurs on a lamp. It may be a reference to some myth or story now lost to us, or it could be symbolic of erotic dreams, as in the case of the medieval succubus, an evil spirit who seduced sleeping men. In any case, it must be seen as a strongly erotic composition.

No doubt there may be other themes which could be included here, but there is one major one to which we must turn before we go on, in the next chapter, to examine the erotic art which is based on ordinary heterosexual lovemaking.

86 A small bronze statuette found in the Thames, of Hermaphrodite holding a folding mirror. 1st–2nd century AD

Though homosexuality is still offensive to many people, a more enlightened attitude is certainly developing. Bestiality is a very different matter, and sexual relationships between humans and other species may seem to many of us something extraordinarily perverse and depraved, connected perhaps mainly with rustics of sub-normal intelligence, and in any case grossly unfair to the innocent members of other animal species which may be involved.

The situation is not quite so clear in classical art, because the mythological implications are so complex. We have seen in an earlier chapter how the animal attributes of various deities were important in their worship and, furthermore, the Greek tendency to envisage a range of hybrid beings which combine the characteristics of an animal and a human leads to such activities as satyrs or Pan mating with goats and deer, behaviour which cannot be more than fifty per cent

87 Marble relief of a shepherd seduced by a siren. Hellenistic or Roman.

bestial for the perpetrators. Centaurs, carrying off mortal women and nymphs with lustful intent are, after all, half-human themselves: though the standard type of centaur in art has his sexual organs at the equine rather than the human end of his body, very early centaurs were human even in this respect. For such hybrids, we should make excuses for some sexual confusion, and remember, too, that the activities of satyrs and centaurs were frequently recorded for entertainment. There is a marked shortage of females of these species, and forays into the realms of mortal and divine women by the males are hardly surprising.

Still in the realms of mythology, we turn to the activities of Zeus (Jupiter), the highest of the Olympian gods. Zeus developed frequent enthusiasms for females other than Hera, his consort, and often carried them through to a successful conclusion in somewhat bizarre ways. His seductions naturally form the subject of many visual representations, not only in antiquity, but also in the Renaissance and later. The story of Leda was especially popular at all periods, and the image of a woman embraced by a swan was clearly considered an acceptably subtle form of eroticism in times which would have rejected many of the more direct depictions we have seen here.

The story of Leda is complicated; as in so many myths, there are many conflicting versions, but it is agreed that she was the mother of the divine twins Castor and Pollux and of Helen. Which of these offspring were fathered by Leda's

88 Leda and the Swan (assisted by a small Cupid) on a Roman lamp. 1st century AD

husband Tyndareus and which by Zeus in the guise of a swan, varies according to different sources. As they were all allegedly conceived on the same night, the confusion is understandable. In some versions, Leda's semi-divine children hatched from eggs, which seems to point very clearly at the swan rather than the human father.

The idea of a human in the embrace of a bird does not at first thought seem especially stimulating, since avian copulation is normally simply a matter of pressing two orifices together; it is perhaps somewhat altered by the realisation that swans are one of only four families of birds (the others are ducks, geese, and the group which includes ostriches, emus and cassowaries) which possess an intromittent organ – to all intents and purposes, a penis. Leda's experience was therefore much the same as any mammalian coitus, and the erotic force of images such as the marble relief (21) or the lamp scenes (88, 89) is correspondingly heightened. Some ancient illustrations of Leda and the swan are relatively low-key, showing her sheltering a very tame and normal-sized swan in the folds of her

89 A fine Athenian lamp of the Roman period decorated with Leda and the Swan. First half of the 3rd century AD

drapery, but the relief illustrated here, which belongs to a standard type of antiquity, is a very powerful piece of work: the Jupiter-swan is of huge size, as befits a deity, and yet entirely a bird, grasping Leda's neck in his bill as so many male animals do in mating. The swan in the lamp scene is less violent, but there is still an undeniable sexual force in the whole scene. One suspects that later artists, even ones as great as Leonardo, found the theme merely a pretty one, a mildly erotic idea (though Michelangelo's Leda is certainly fairly abandoned to sensual pleasure), but the classical tradition contains a far more passionate strand. The poet Yeats recognised this in his poem on the subject. I have dwelt on the theme of Leda and the swan in some detail, partly because it is a very frequent image in classical art, and partly to illustrate how quickly, in seriously considering this myth of an animal-god overpowering a mortal woman, one forgets the initial reaction to the idea of 'bestiality'.

Zeus ravished other females in such sexually unsatisfactory forms as clouds and showers of gold, but his liaison with Europa was also in animal form, and

90 A lamp with a scene of a woman on a bed with a small horse or pony; made in Athens by the lamp-maker Preimos in the middle of the third century AD

there are pictures from archaic to late-Roman times of the god carrying her off, in the form of a beautiful white bull. For some reason, after carrying Europa away to Crete, Zeus shifted shape yet again before completing his designs upon her, and it was in the form of an eagle that he consummated this particular affair. Whether this was a disappointment to Europa or a relief seems uncertain. The scenes of Europa and the bull are not, therefore, truly erotic in themselves, as they describe only the prelude to the sexual episode.

While Leda's relations with the swan clearly belong in the realm of mythology, there are a few other illustrations of sexual connection between species which do not; those shown here all occur on the discus scenes of Roman lamps, a rich source of erotic imagery. The Athenian lamp of the Roman period (90) is a particularly fine one, of the same type as one of the Leda lamps (89). It shows a woman on a bed with a small horse. There are similar scenes involving asses or mules, and dogs, all with women. One would suppose that bestiality as an actual sexual aberration is probably more common between human males and females of other species than between women and male quadrupeds, if only because it would be easier for a man to force another animal to submit to sexual penetration

91 A Roman lamp with a fanciful erotic scene, probably a parody, showing a woman and a crocodile; the design may be a satirical reference to Cleopatra VII of Egypt. 1st century AD

than it would be for a woman to arouse a male animal sufficiently for the purpose. Yet a number of representations of women with animals on lamps are matched by only one figure-type of a man copulating with an animal (a donkey). The precise intention of these scenes is uncertain, and they may be humorous or satirical, though even if this is the case, one may suppose that they were also intended to be titillating.

Groups such as this, especially where they involve women with horses or donkeys, should possibly be considered in relation to stories such as the *Golden Ass* of Lucius Apuleius, written in the second century AD. Apuleius's story is not original, and inferior versions by other authors survive, so the tale may be regarded as a well-known one in the Roman world. It is written in the first person, and is an account of Lucius's metamorphosis into an ass, brought about by his meddling with witchcraft, and his eventual return to human shape through the aid of the goddess Isis. While Lucius is trapped in the body of a donkey, he has various adventures which include a torrid love-affair with an aristocratic woman. It is the lady who seduces him, but the liaison is described as being gratifying to both parties. Lucius's owner, impressed by his amatory performance, decides to make money by exhibiting him in public, copulating with a condemned murderess (his mistress could not be expected to lower her social status by appearing in public in this manner). The shocked animal cannot face such degradation, and makes good his escape. It is reasonable to suppose that such public exhibitions did take place – there is no doubt that they have done in very recent times. To some men, the idea of connection between a woman and a male animal is apparently very exciting. In any case, scenes such as those on the lamps may at the very least refer to stories like the *Golden Ass*.

92 Red-figure cup by Epiktetos: a maenad offers herself to a mule, one of the Dionysiac animals. This is the other side of the cup shown in 67. Last quarter of the 6th century BC

93 Red-figure cup by the Brygos Painter
with an orgy scene which includes a
woman being beaten with a slipper.
*c.*480 BC

26 *left* A satyr
copulating with a buck,
as decoration on a
black-figure cup. *c.*520
BC

27 *left* A black-figure
amphora with a scene of
men and youths
courting; painted by the
Painter of Berlin 1686.
*c.*540 BC

28 *right* A man and boy
on a black-figure vase.
Late 6th century BC

29 Pan uncovering Hermaphrodite: a
wall-painting from Pompeii. 1st century
AD

94 Cast of a Greek gem engraved with a cockerel treading a hen. 5th–4th century BC

Another lamp scene somewhat remotely connected with the above depicts two animals of very different species copulating, a donkey mounting a lion. This is almost certainly straight parody, probably of the common image of a beast of prey overpowering an ass, goat or other unfortunate creature. There are also a few scenes of normal animal mating, such as the pair of birds in 94. These are at the most borderline eroticism, and perhaps better regarded as simple genre scenes.

Before we leave this subject of minority sexual interests, it is worth mentioning one which is virtually absent in both Greek and Roman art. One of the most striking features of English pornography of the eighteenth and nineteenth centuries, both in written and graphic form, is the obsession with flagellation. It is a constantly recurring motif, and its acceptance contrasts strangely with the revulsion aroused by male homosexuality in many of these works. Whipping is, of course, a feature of many religious practices, including some aspects of Christianity, and there is plenty of evidence that it formed part of many ancient religious rites. Furthermore, whipping as punishment, especially of disobedient slaves and children, was standard practice. There seems no obvious reason, therefore, why whipping as a sexual activity should not be as common in ancient art as it was in recent times. In fact, as an erotic motif, it appears to be absent from both Greek and Roman imagery. There is the occasional smack with a slipper on Greek painted pottery, and females often threaten importunate lovers, above all satyrs, with weapons which happen to be to hand, but there is nothing in the purely sexual range of behaviour to compare with the carefully selected and enthusiastically wielded bundles of birch twigs which so inspired Victorian voluptuaries. There was plenty of non-sexual violence in Roman life and indeed in Greek, but recent times have not been deficient in this respect. Perhaps one should conclude that a repressive attitude to sexuality is particularly conducive to this taste, combining pleasure and punishment in a way which satisfies both the desire and the guilt. The more natural and hearty approach of antiquity is a refreshing contrast.

Above Scene of two lovers on a bed from a
bronze mirror cover (see also the colour
illustration 35). 1st century AD

previous page Symposium scene with two
pairs of lovers from a red-figure vase by
the Dikaios Painter (see also the colour
illustration 31). Late 6th century BC

We have now arrived at the major category of truly erotic illustrations on Greek and Roman artefacts, those which, without any religious, humorous or satirical intent, depict sexual activities between heterosexual couples. As in the case of some of the scenes discussed in the previous chapter, it is very often entirely a matter of personal judgement whether any given image is intended solely for erotic enjoyment, or whether it may have some other meaning. If we are to draw any conclusions of interest from the types of scene represented, we have to consider factors such as the apparent feelings of the characters shown by the ancient artists; some of our impressions may well be mistaken, but they are worth recording provided nobody regards them as proven facts, but as opinions.

Scenes of heterosexual intercourse are fairly common in Greek and Roman art, though the Greek evidence is almost entirely on painted pottery, a fact which has certain social and other implications. In the case of Roman material, erotic decoration occurs on a range of objects broadly similar to that which we have already seen, decorated ceramics in particular. We know that in antiquity erotic scenes were sometimes the subject of paintings, but those which survive, all of them Roman, are not the work of celebrated artists. Erotic themes are also found in some Roman sculpture, terracotta figurines and lamps, and small bronze utensils such as mirrors and knife-handles. Though phallic motifs were common as personal ornaments because of their lucky qualities, jewellery with truly erotic decoration seems to be very rare: there are a few engraved gems with erotic scenes, though not as many as some of the eighteenth- and nineteenth-century collectors would have us believe. Both portable paintings and wall-paintings are likely to have been used primarily in situations where they were especially apposite to the surroundings, but small articles of use like knives and lamps would hardly have been confined to some special circumstances if they had erotic decoration. One must inevitably conclude that scenes of lovemaking were acceptable in their own right. Objects such as mirrors and mirror-cases were for feminine use, but the material which is most commonly decorated with erotic subjects in an Athenian context would have been used mainly by men. The Attic painted pottery in question consists of vessels used in the service of wine, especially the *kylix* (pl. *kylikes*), the drinking-cup in the form of an elegant shallow bowl with a slender stem and two handles. Mixing-bowls, large wine-containers, jugs and wine-coolers are also vessels which can be decorated in this way. They would have been used at the type of party, the symposium, which is depicted in so many of the erotic paintings themselves. I shall shortly return to the subject of the symposium in greater detail.

Erotic scenes which show human couples as opposed to mythological subjects occur in other cultures related to that of Greece; in the case of Etruscan examples, there is also a link with the later developments in Roman art, as there is, naturally, between Greek and Roman. There are sexual scenes in some Etruscan tomb-paintings, and carvings of this nature on stone sarcophagi, both funerary contexts. This implies some religious significance perhaps; we have already seen that the apotropaic power of the phallus may be invoked in connection with death, and this is probably related. While erotic scenes, like all representational subjects, are virtually absent from the art of the Iron Age Celts, appearing first in the Celtic areas during the Roman Empire, they do occur in a contemporary culture which has links both with the Celts and with Greek and Etruscan civilisation. The Iron Age inhabitants of the area round the head of the Adriatic –

north-eastern Italy, Austria and Yugoslavia – had a distinctive art style which is found on their decorated bronze *situlae* (wine-buckets). These are richly ornamented in relief with friezes of animals, hunting and combat scenes, processions and banquets, all themes which are familiar enough in Greek art of the period. The banquet scenes occasionally include a couple on a bed, but whether the motif is meant simply as a domestic one, or has some ritual significance, it is impossible to say with our limited knowledge of these peoples. The situlae, like Greek painted pottery, would obviously have been used at convivial gatherings.

The range of settings in which lovemaking is presented in Greek and Roman art is fairly wide, but it is not always easy to tell exactly how we should interpret them. Some give every impression of being purely domestic, illustrating sexual activity as an aspect of everyday life. As we shall see, this seems to be more common in Roman than in Greek contexts. At the other end of the scale are the objects which may depict sex as an entertainment for onlookers. Many Roman lamps with sexual scenes show dwarfs engaging in these activities (96), and it seems very likely that we have here a reference to public performances which would have appealed to the rather jaded tastes of some sections of Roman society. It must be remembered that many Roman lamps bear pictures of other forms of public entertainment, especially gladiatorial contests, and we have seen that

95 A scene on a bronze mirror cover of two lovers. This is the reverse of the mirror cover in illustration 112. Mid-4th century BC

some of the bestiality themes noted in the previous chapter may well also refer to staged performances. The proportions of many of the figures in the erotic types on lamps suggests that they are dwarfs (not children, as has occasionally been asserted): in many cultures, people with certain types of physical abnormality have best been able to earn their living in the world of entertainment, and dwarfs have tended to be especially popular in this respect.

Perhaps the most important setting implied for sexual activities, at least on Greek pottery, is the symposium. Even here, there is a considerable range of context shown, from the single couple, confined in the small circular decorated field within the cup, to the painted frieze surrounding the vessel, which may depict an orgy with numerous participants. The Athenian symposium (*symposion*) was a drinking and talking-party which, according to circumstances, seems to have ranged from a philosophical discussion-group of the most intellectually exalted kind to a no-holds-barred drunken orgy. One of the important factors is that the Greeks, unlike the Romans, did not drink with their meals, so that wine-drinking became a separate activity, accompanied at the most by small snacks. It is true that the wine was heavily watered, hence the mixing-bowl or *krater*: both Greeks and Romans regarded the consumption of neat wine as the very mark of the barbarian, and sneered at people such as the Celts who practised it. Nevertheless, however generously diluted the wine may have been, the evidence of the vase-paintings themselves confirms that on occasion, enough of it was consumed to render the guests very drunk indeed. Intoxication did not have the same stigma attached to it as has been usual in many later societies, perhaps partly because of the religious significance of drunkenness in the rites of Dionysos. One cannot help wondering if the

96 A lamp showing dwarfs in a lovemaking scene, perhaps a public performance. 1st century AD

conversation at many symposia was as brilliant as the guests imagined at the time.

Though the invited guests at a Greek symposium were all male, since respectable women were excluded from this kind of social activity, as from so much else, females could be present in other capacities: entertainments were often provided, and vase-paintings show scantily clad or even completely naked flute-girls and dancers, as well as hetairai, who could take part in so many things denied to the Greek wife. Hetairai were not simply prostitutes – there is a separate word, *porne*, for the ordinary whore – but were women of some culture and education, often foreigners. They would have been able and expected to take part in the conversation at such a party, but both they and the entertainers might eventually find themselves called upon to provide sexual services to the men present.

The equivalent Roman social gathering differed in many respects, even though wealthy Romans in consciously hellenising periods such as the early Empire probably liked to think that they were continuing a tradition and perpetuating all that was best in Greek culture. The influence of the Etruscans is almost certainly a major factor in the character of the Roman symposium. Romans of the Republican period, who often had a decidedly severe and puritanical approach to life, were fond of deploring the freedom of Etruscan women, who, amongst other forms of allegedly reprehensible behaviour, mixed socially with men and took part in banquets and parties, reclining on the festive couches with their male partners. However much early Romans deprecated this conduct, it became the norm in their own society. Cornelius Nepos, a writer of the first century BC, remarks that the main contrast between Greek and Roman women is that the former sit secluded in the interior parts of the house, while the latter accompany their husbands to dinner-parties. It is important to note that these gatherings, in spite of some heavy drinking, had now become dinner-parties rather than drinking-parties. Satirists such as Petronius and Juvenal paint a grim picture of

97 A symposium scene depicted on a red-figure cup by the Nikosthenes Painter. One of the young men is holding a double-ended *olisbos* (dildo), and another of these objects is hanging on the wall. Late 6th century BC

98 A small terracotta vessel, probably made in Campania, in the form of a couple reclining together on a couch. 2nd–1st century BC

some of these events, ranging from mere vulgar and ludicrous ostentation to disgusting excess, but while there must have been occasional justification for such a view, there is no reason to believe that such sordid parties were common. On the contrary, a Roman dinner-party at which both sexes mixed and conversed, as they did at its Etruscan forerunner, may seem more civilised to many modern tastes than the male-club atmosphere of the Athenian symposium, however fine the intellectual level of the latter may have been at its very best. It is easy to see that the male-dominated culture of Victorian Britain experienced in this, as in so many other things, a fellow-feeling with the Greeks and a certain discomfort in the presence of the Romans.

If we now consider the actual scenes depicted on objects, we find that there are several ways of categorising them. The most obvious is to deal with them chronologically, but this scheme makes it more difficult to appreciate some of the interesting similarities and contrasts between Greek work and Roman, so I propose instead to start with the most restrained and low-key depictions of lovemaking, and move up to the more uninhibited and explicit. It may come as something of a surprise to many to find Roman art well represented in the former category and Greek in the latter; this is something to which I shall return later.

In defining 'restrained' or 'low-key' erotic images, I am excluding those which show affection or love without a specifically sexual content. There are, for

99 An embracing
couple on a black-figure
vase by the Acheloos
Painter; the other side of
the vase illustrated as
13. Late 6th century BC

example, Roman terracotta figurines which are of a standing, fully clothed couple embracing and kissing, and there are also items of jewellery – rings and pendants – which are decorated with kissing couples. These, like the motif of a pair of clasped hands, refer to marriage or betrothal, and though they may be said to contain a potential erotic force, they differ from my first category, which may be defined as illustrations of specifically sexual situations incorporating love or affection as a definite part of the theme. A significant degree of artistic skill is required to depict sexual activity and still convey emotional elements. The observer's own judgement may also vary, and I can only indicate those images which seem to me to concern emotional as well as physical attraction.

The first example is perhaps a borderline case, but if it is accepted, it must rank as one of the finest ancient expressions of eroticism, combining love and desire. It is a small pipeclay figurine (100) made in Gaul in the second century AD, and found at Bordeaux. It shows a couple in bed, with their pet dog curled up on the blanket at their feet, a thoroughly domestic scene. The fact that the pair are in

100 A Gallo-Roman terracotta found at Bordeaux, of a couple in bed with their dog lying at their feet. 2nd century AD

bed, and that they are exchanging caresses, seems to justify the inclusion of the piece in the class of erotic representations. The great importance of this little model, the work of a Gallo-Roman artist, lies in the fact that it exhibits a tenderness, realism and sensitivity which has no parallel and no equal in surviving Greek erotic art. We must not forget the bias of our sources, since the Greek material does not illustrate this domestic type of situation, but the fact that it is illustrated in provincial Roman art is striking in itself.

Perhaps even more notable is the fact that this gentle and tender manner towards sexual themes is also seen on the class of Roman artefact which most closely parallels Greek painted pottery. Arretine pottery was made, like Attic painted ware, for use at the parties of the rich. It was manufactured during the early years of the Roman Empire, the best decorated ware belonging to the reign of the Emperor Augustus, and like all art of the Augustan period it displays obvious signs of conscious hellenising. The technique of producing the low-relief ornament is one of mass production, the figures being made as punches which were stamped into pottery moulds in which the final pots were formed. Provincial samian ware was made in the same way, but the use of the decorative motifs tends to be far more haphazard on the latter: Arretine bowls frequently have decorative

themes which form a logical whole round the pot, perhaps a hunting scene or mythological tale, and sometimes a symposium scene showing couples reclining together on couches, as both Greeks and Romans did on such occasions. It is interesting to see that the Arretine figure-types, mass-produced though they were, seem more subtle and graceful than many of the equivalent illustrations on Attic red-figure. This is probably due primarily to the exquisite workmanship of the Roman pottery, but one may also suspect that there was a real difference of atmosphere in the type of party being depicted.

Erotic themes were frequently produced in the workshop of Marcus Perennius, the leading manufacturer of Arretine at its very best period. The consummate skill of the artist who made the Perennius figure-types was such that he could make it perfectly clear that actual lovemaking was taking place, while keeping the postures completely natural, with the genitals of the figures out of sight of the onlooker. This reticence is the result of realism and artistic skill rather than modesty, and is not usually found in other types of Roman ceramics which follow the Arretine tradition, or even in the work of Arretine workshops less outstanding than that of Perennius.

Gaulish samian ware is one of these derivatives, and 103 is an example of an erotic type found on Central Gaulish work of the later second century AD, over a hundred and fifty years later than the elegant creations of Marcus Perennius. The

101, 102 A mould for the manufacture of an Arretine vase, made in the workshop of Marcus Perennius. The decoration consists of pairs of lovers in various poses. Late 1st century BC

103 An erotic figure-type occasionally used on Central Gaulish samian ware in the second century AD; it is influenced by Arretine ware, but is considerably less accomplished.

104 A jug of Knidian relief-decorated ware with figure-types of lovers. Late 1st–2nd century AD

brilliant technique of the Arretine potter is lacking, and it is hard to judge whether the scene is intended to convey sexual enjoyment alone, or some emotional impact as well. The pose, though explicit and slightly awkward, does at least bring the faces of the two characters close, a convention which hints at some warmth of feeling. Samian ware is characteristic of the northern and western provinces of the Roman Empire, but at the same period, pottery with erotic scenes was being produced at the other end of the Empire: 104 illustrates a Knidian pottery jug (Knidos is in the area which is now Turkey), which is part of the same tradition and displays a degree of artistry about on a par with that of the Gaulish products.

If we search for similarly affectionate motifs on Greek material, we find few. Probably one of the most gentle and expressive scenes is that on a small red-figure jug now in Berlin (34). This depicts a very young couple, gazing fixedly into each other's eyes; the youth is seated, and the girl is about to settle herself astride his lap. The way in which the lovers are isolated on the black background accentuates their concentration on each other. This is not a symposium scene, as far as we can see, but something more private and deeply felt.

The young men and women in 31, on the other hand, are certainly at a symposium, but as in the Arretine bowls, it seems possible to sense something more than sexual excitement alone; the warmth of the embraces contrasts with the apparently rather perfunctory contacts so often seen in these paintings. The isolation of one couple can heighten the potential affection in an image, and as the Greek kylix usually has a circular area of decoration within the bowl, there are many such couples on the painted pottery. It is therefore surprising that so few of them seem to radiate the kind of warmth which is undeniably present in the Arretine figures. One of the factors may be eye-contact: it is easier to give an impression of attachment between two figures if they are looking at each other, yet even where they are (105, 106) the atmosphere conveyed is lively and cheerful rather than intense and emotional. The paintings within the kylikes seem to relate very definitely to the symposium scenes in the surrounding friezes, indicating a hearty enjoyment of sex for its own sake.

Some of the communal activities depicted on Greek vases become hearty in the extreme, and in some cases they remind one of much Victorian pornography, which is often tremendously busy and energetic. The examples which go furthest in this direction are those, like 107 and 108, in which the women have to cope with more than one male each. As one might expect in these circumstances, these rather hectic conjunctions begin to look more like hard work than pleasure: even the men sometimes look serious almost to the point of gloominess, as on the beautifully painted vessel in the Louvre (110). There are occasional signs of unwillingness amongst the female participants; a crouching girl in an orgy scene by the Brygos painter (108) seems to be fending off her partner.

It is possible that erotic pictures with this orgiastic element may be satirically intended, but it is very unlikely when one considers their use. They are far more likely to have been designed to inflame amorous feelings at the parties where the vessels were used, and we can therefore assume that they accurately reflect the kind of activity which upper-class Athenian men tended to find exciting. The subordinate role of the women seems very evident throughout, yet the paintings have a freshness and honesty which makes them very attractive. It is worth noting that, as in the case of the Arretine ware, this type of decoration was executed by some of the finest and most celebrated artists in the medium: it was

105, 106 Two red-figure cups by the
Triptolemos Painter, with very similar
lovemaking scenes. c.470 BC

30 *right* An Arretine vase, with a figure-
type of lovers. Late 1st century BC

33 *above* A black-figure stand, decorated with a pair of lovers. Second half of the 6th century BC

31 *above left* A red-figure vase by the Dikaios Painter, with a symposium scene. Late 6th century BC

32 *left* A Campanian red-figure vase by the CA Painter, decorated with a symposium scene. Second half of the 4th century BC

not a genre to which inferior craftsmen turned to help their sales, but one which the best could be proud of.

It would be possible from the available material to compile a list of positions for copulation, and indeed this has been done, both in antiquity and modern times. While an exhaustive list has little purpose, there may perhaps be some interest in considering the matter in general, though any inferences about the significance of various postures must be drawn with the greatest care. It has already been noted that artistic considerations come into this. It is hardly to be supposed that the artists and craftsmen who produced erotic designs were attempting a sociological study of the sexual customs of their culture; they were producing images which conveyed the idea of sex as clearly and straightforwardly as they could within the normal artistic conventions in which they had grown up. If the aim is to arouse sexual feeling in the onlooker – and this must be the aim of many of these scenes – some positions of coitus can be visually ambiguous and lacking in impact. The common 'missionary position' is one. Very skilled artists can convey the nature of the activity by facial expression and nuances of posture (30), but it is easier to be unambiguous by resorting to positions which can mean nothing but sexual intercourse to any reasonable person, for example the popular Greek rear-entry poses (109, 111), or by showing the genitals clearly in contact,

34 *left* A scene on a red-figure jug by the Shuvalov Painter. The seated youth and the girl about to climb onto his lap are shown isolated against the black background. Last quarter of the 5th century BC

107 Red-figure cup by the Pedeius Painter, with a very energetic orgy scene. Late 6th century BC

108 Another detail of the decoration on the cup by the Brygos Painter, no.93: the girl in the centre appears to be slightly unwilling. c.480 BC

or about to be so. It is therefore important to bear in mind that the choice of pose may not depend chiefly on what was customary in actual sexual practice at the time, but on what would be of greatest interest to the customer and could be most vividly illustrated by the artist.

With this in mind, we can nevertheless note some of the positions and types of activity which are depicted, and consider whether they may tell us anything about the tastes and sexual preferences and preoccupations of the Greeks and Romans who bought and used the decorated objects. It is immediately striking that there is a high proportion of rear-entry couplings recorded by the Greek vase-painters, with the female standing or kneeling. This rather impersonal stance tends to be more gratifying to the man than the woman. Professor Dover (*Greek Homosexuality*) considers that many of these depict anal rather than vaginal penetration, but it seems to me that it is quite impossible to make a judgement of this kind. In the side views shown, it would be extremely difficult to tell even in a photograph, let alone a drawing, precisely what was taking place in any given example, and any of these paintings could just as easily show normal coitus. Remembering that the women in these pictures are hetairai, it is true that anal connection would, as Dover suggests, have had the advantage of being effectively contraceptive. Furthermore, if nineteenth-century pornography is any guide,

109 *left* A red-figure cup by the Briseis Painter. The position is perhaps more satisfactory for the male partner than for the female. 500–475 BC

110 *right* A red-figure *stamnos* by Polygnotos, with some rather solemn revellers. *c*.430 BC

high-spirited sexual romps such as those on many of the Greek pots often lead to experiment with variants on straightforward copulation. On the other hand, hetairai must have been able to cope with the hazard of pregnancy, since they are often enough shown indulging in normal intercourse, so the contraceptive theory has little weight. Anal coitus is not likely to be associated with homosexual experience or preference amongst the males in these orgies, since it is no more a norm in homosexual relationships than it is in heterosexual ones. It is true that the practice is mentioned in Greek literature, but as we have seen, the mode of male-to-male lovemaking normally illustrated on pottery is quite different. All in all, it cannot be demonstrated that these frequent rear-entry connections are other than normal. What they do seem to convey very strongly is the atmosphere of the orgy, with the men using the women as the fancy takes them, rather than the atmosphere of private and personal relationships. This is naturally what one might expect in the circumstances. The ambience is as far removed as possible from the Gallo-Roman couple in their bed with the family dog at their feet.

Rear-entry positions are also quite frequent in Roman work, but they are seldom standing ones, except in the few (17) where there is a ritual element, the male figure being a satyr rather than a human. More commonly, the couple is shown on a bed, with the man kneeling, so that the impression is not so strongly that of a very fleeting contact. Another rear-entry position which appears in Roman and some later Greek examples is the lying-down rear-entry, which when seen from the front, affords a very detailed view of the proceedings. Examples are

111 A red-figure cup by Douris, with another variation of the rear-entry approach. 500–470 BC

134

the Boston mirror-cover (112), another mirror-cover of later date, first century AD, in Rome (35), and the small bronze knife-handle (113), which being three-dimensional does not need to have selected this position simply in order to be explicit. Variants also occur on pottery, some of them strained and rather unnatural, perhaps due at least in part to lack of competence in the craftsman. The popularity of the position in art must be due to a great extent to its visual effectiveness.

As one might expect, face-to-face positions with the male above occur with some frequency, but various devices are used to heighten the erotic impact by

112 A bronze mirror-cover from Corinth, decorated with an erotic scene. This is a position which is particularly clear in a two-dimensional, or low-relief, representation. Mid-4th century BC

113 Bronze Roman knife-handle in the form of a pair of lovers. Erotic themes were not uncommon as decoration for small handles of this kind.

making the male genitals at least partially visible. A side view of this posture where both partners are fully stretched out makes little impression as an erotic image, but there are some entertaining versions of the classic missionary position in Etruscan art of the seventh century BC and contemporary situla art, where the problem has been solved by the naive expedient of having the male figure apparently hovering in mid-air over the supine female. This will not do, however, for the more sophisticated work of the Attic vase-painters or for the Romans. A variant face-to-face position which is seen in a number of red-figure paintings is that in which the woman has her legs raised onto the man's shoulders, so that her thighs do not obstruct the observer's view of his body. As it happens, this is another mode which in real life is generally more pleasant for the male than for his partner: for the woman, it can be extremely uncomfortable, compressing the rib-cage and making breathing difficult, as well as bringing about an angle of penetration that can be painful. Confirmation of the fact that it was enjoyed by Greek men is found in *Lysistrata*, where it seems to figure in the catechism of delights which Lysistrata makes her followers swear to deny their husbands: 'I won't raise up my Persian slippers towards the ceiling'. Roman versions tend to favour a more natural pose (for example the Arretine figure-type, *30*), though at least one of the Pompeian wall-paintings has the feet-on-shoulder pose; however, in that case, the woman is shown sitting on the edge of a bed, and the man standing, which is a far less exhausting version. It is hard to say to what extent purely visual considerations affect the choice in this range of positions.

Greek pottery has a fair number of examples of the woman-astride theme, but this is especially common in Roman art. Indeed, on objects such as Roman lamps,

35 Lovers on a bed decorating a bronze mirror-cover. This relief is full of fascinating detail, from the erotic picture hanging on the wall and the puppy on a stool by the bed, to the woman's jewellery and elaborate hairstyle. 1st century AD

36 *above* A small marble relief from
Pompeii depicting a pair of lovers. Mid-1st
century AD

37 *right* A Roman wall-painting of lovers
from Pompeii. 1st century AD

38 A wall-painting of lovers from
Pompeii. 1st century AD

it is probably true to say that the position in which the male reclines and the female squats above him, either facing him or with her back to his face, is the most characteristic of all. All variants of this approach, whether the man is lying back or sitting, give a good deal of freedom to the female partner and require her very active co-operation. It is even said by some that there are men who feel at a psychological disadvantage in such encounters because they see the woman as the dominant partner. From the artistic point of view, it is possible to make the action very clear by having the genitals of both figures visible. It is tempting to speculate that the frequency of this type of position on Roman objects implies rather more freedom of choice among the women than we see in Greek contexts, but such a conclusion would be stretching the evidence too far. All we can say is that woman-astride positions were erotically stimulating to those who wanted sexual decoration on items such as lamps.

We have already seen that orgies in which several people take part together are by no means infrequent on Attic painted pottery. In particular, the hetairai and the slave musicians and dancers who were present seem to have been called upon to satisfy more than one of the men at once. There seem to be few Roman images of this kind. Even the Pompeian wall-paintings depict single couples, any supernumerary characters merely observing, rather than taking any part in the action. There are a few lamp and samian figure-types which show couples physically supported or egged on by additional individuals, but again, the latter do not seem to be sexually aroused themselves, so these scenes do not convey the atmosphere of an orgy. Obviously the small circular area provided by the discus of a lamp is barely adequate to show the complex communal activities seen in some of the red-figure vases, and it is also true that painting is a far easier medium for such a purpose than the low-relief modelling produced in moulds. All the same, we can be sure that if craftsmen of the quality of those employed in the factory of Marcus Perennius had wished to represent a frieze of figures engaged in complex sexual conjugations, they could easily have done so; instead, the Arretine symposia have pairs of figures so absorbed in each other that one doubts whether they would have been conscious of the other couples at all. It is only fair to stress that this does not constitute evidence of a lack of orgies in Roman society – any more than the Greek scenes are evidence of their taking place in Athens: the paintings could be mere wishful thinking, like many of the Victorian descriptions of orgies. What we *can* reasonably infer is that the Greek customer for an erotically decorated pot was more likely to be stimulated by the idea of multi-person sexual contact than was his Roman counterpart. Could this, again, be due to the attitude to women? It is tempting to draw such conclusions, but perhaps unwise.

The cheerful and rather athletic approach to sex which we sense in much of the Greek material is best paralleled on Roman objects on the lamps and products such as the late Gallo-Roman pottery with relief-decorated medallions, made in the Rhône valley. As I remarked earlier, some of these scenes could depict sex-shows rather than private activities. In some of them, the couples have props such as lamps or swords, which they wave aloft, and on the Rhône valley medallions (114), there is often a comment or exhortation inscribed on the scene. These are usually difficult to understand without a knowledge of sexual terminology and slang in Latin, but the general gist is obvious enough. It is also on lamps and Rhône valley vessels that we most commonly see examples of the practice of

116 *above* Roman lamp with a *soixante-neuf* pose: though there are some modern forgeries showing this type of pose, ancient examples are rare.
1st century AD

114 *below* Lovemaking scenes on moulded pottery medallions, which decorate pots made in the Rhône Valley region of France in the later Roman period.

115 *right* A Roman lamp with a fellatio
scene: this is perhaps more common in
Greek than in Roman representations.
1st century AD

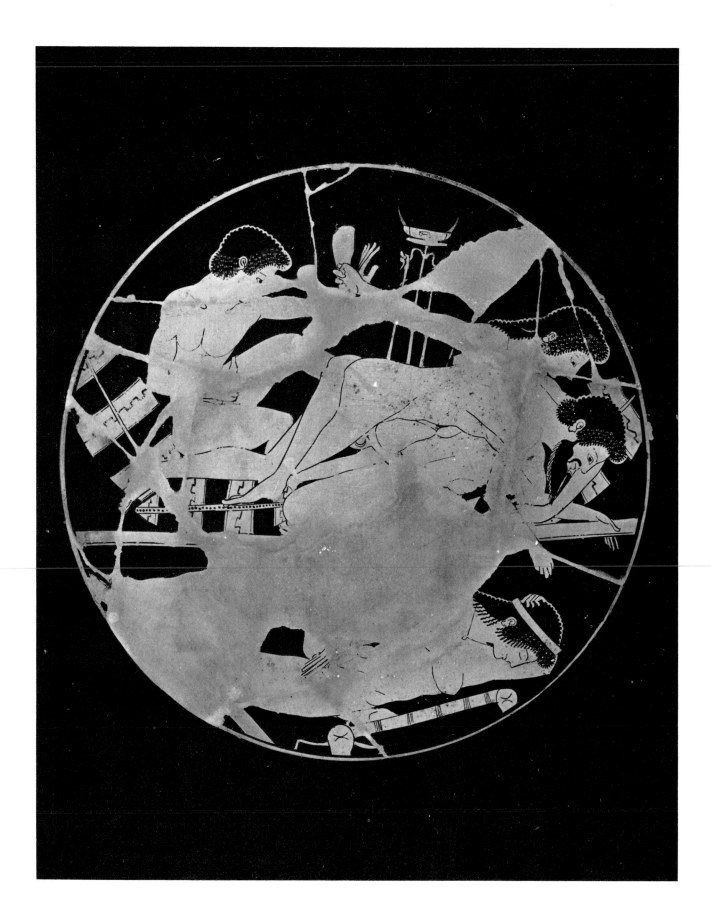

117 *left* Red-figure cup by the Thalia Painter. The damage to the vessel makes the details of this scene somewhat uncertain. One of the girls is wielding a slipper, while the other appears to be asleep on the floor beneath the couch. Late 6th century BC

118 *below* A small beaker in Central Gaulish colour-coated ware ('black samian ware') with a variety of erotic scenes, including a masturbating man. First quarter of the 2nd century AD

fellatio, which is also quite often depicted on Greek red-figure. Cunnilingus is extremely rare; literary evidence suggests that the Greeks, at any rate, regarded it with revulsion. There is a Roman lamp type (116) which seems to depict a *soixante-neuf* pose, but it is exceptional. Forgers of ancient lamps in the eighteenth and nineteenth centuries attempted to fill this gap by providing more such scenes, and have therefore clouded the issue somewhat.

We mentioned masturbation in an earlier chapter as behaviour more usually associated with satyrs than humans. I do not know of a single visual image of female masturbation in Greek or Roman material, though it is certainly mentioned in literature; both the writers and the artists were normally men. The dildo-wielding hetairai on Greek vases are clearly entertaining their customers: in

many cases, they are almost certainly performing a lascivious dance, and the closest modern parallels could undoubtedly be found in strip-tease shows. A red-figure scene which is often quoted as showing masturbation is one which has a couple on a couch with a sleeping hetaira on the floor beneath, her hand resting on her belly (117). One may, of course, speculate about the activities which have left her in this exhausted state, but as painted, she is not indulging in anything more than slumber.

There is one intriguing example of male masturbation illustrated on samian ware, on a small beaker in so-called black samian, made in the workshop of a potter called Libertus at Lezoux during the first two decades of the second century AD. The beaker is decorated with several rather formalised small erotic reliefs of the type which may ultimately be derived from comedy, but there is one figure of a seated slave holding a lantern: he is a common enough figure, but here, amongst the riot of erotica with which he is surrounded, he has been subtly altered in the mould to suggest that he is joining in the spirit of the activity, though lacking a partner (118).

The overall picture which emerges for both Greek and Roman material is a matter-of-factness and casualness in illustrating these erotic themes which is very foreign to us, but exactly what we might expect, in view of the different threshold of embarrassment and shame which the ancients would have had. The Greek material displays little sign of emotional involvement among the participants: the pottery is aimed at a particular clientèle, and a particular context, where it would be surprising if it did. It is noteworthy that the lack of embarrassment in the Greek painted pottery extends beyond the illustration of erotic themes; it was considered acceptable to depict excretion and even the more repulsive and disgraceful results of overindulgence in drink.

The erotic decoration on Roman objects is far less restricted socially than Greek. Although Arretine vessels, and the rare examples of silver tableware which have comparable decoration, were undoubtedly intended for the use of the rich, clay oil-lamps were not, and they are a major vehicle for this type of ornament. What is particularly striking is that the allegedly crude and cruel society of the Roman Empire seems to have been able to summon up a more gentle and emotional approach to the subject than the Greeks, along with a similarly light-hearted attitude implied by the probability of public sex-shows. In every way, the Roman material seems to cover a broader scope, and to accept themes connected with sex in a very wide range of contexts.

As I have already suggested, the effect on the sensibilities of the acceptance of phallic motifs in art, for reasons which are not sexual at all, nevertheless paves the way for a calm attitude towards intentionally erotic material. The Victorians were quite right to fear that exposure to 'impropriety' blunts the fine edge of one's shockability. Mysteries are bound to be more terrifying than known facts, and the *idea* of an everyday utensil with an erotic picture on it is far more startling than the actuality.

Conclusions

In the foregoing chapters we have seen something of the range of sexual imagery in classical art, and have tried to assess its meaning and significance to the cultures which created and used it. It remains to summarise these conclusions briefly, and also, since the study of this type of material is still fraught with difficulties, to comment on the necessity and importance of giving these objects their due weight in any discussion of the past.

The first point to note is that overtly sexual representations were *common* in both Greek and Roman art. They are to be found on a wide range of artefacts, including many which were articles of everyday use, such as Roman clay lamps. It is therefore perfectly clear that their use was not restricted to sexual situations. Though many objects are still made with decoration of an erotic kind, and were made even in the most puritan periods of the nineteenth century, they are intended for very restricted use: even where their main purpose is humorous, as is often the case, most people would be very cautious about displaying them, and would first make certain that those to whom they wished to show them were more likely to be amused than shocked.

We have suggested that the ancient objects with sexually explicit ornament were not all made for purposes which can properly be termed 'erotic', that is, to provide sexual stimulation, but that in fact they fall into several quite distinct categories. One of the major classes is to be explained in connection with the religious beliefs and rites of the Graeco-Roman world. As in so many other societies, fertility was a matter of prime importance, and there were many gods and goddesses who were particularly concerned with it. This association with fertility can hardly be adequately expressed without recourse to sexual symbolism of some kind, and many of the deities involved had attributes, or were worshipped with rituals, which included elements that seem to us straightforwardly sexual. Where such attributes and imagery concentrate on the theme of motherhood, they appear acceptable and even attractive to modern western thought, but where male sexuality is brought in, the imagery was universally regarded in the recent past as obscene, and is still viewed with the utmost uneasiness by many who regard themselves as tolerant today.

The rites performed in the worship of one of the gods concerned with fertility are of special importance. Dionysos, though chiefly thought of as the god of wine, had broader powers, and the mythical entourage which is so often depicted in his iconography contains many outspokenly phallic representations. Furthermore, the worship of this deity is the source of drama, and Greek comedy gives ample evidence of this sexual element. The very roots of all European drama are firmly planted in this phallic worship.

A fairly minor religious element which also disturbed earlier scholars was that of healing shrines, and the existence of votive offerings in a form which seemed to them improper. Considerably more widespread, however, was the existence of phallic objects and representations which had a more peripherally religious meaning, as amulets to keep misfortune at bay. The importance of the image of the phallus, and some other sexual motifs, as apotropaic devices probably stems originally from fertility cults, but their development can be seen more as a superstitious practice than a seriously religious one. Phallic amulets were worn, and phallic symbols displayed in public places, to keep off the Evil Eye: they were not intended to be sexually titillating. Modern versions of them, together with gestures which are likewise phallic or sexual in origin, are still common, especially in Mediterranean countries, and have the same purpose.

Two other classes of sexual imagery have been described. One is difficult to identify and, in some cases, to separate from other classes, namely material which was intended to be humorous. It is not always easy to appreciate the humour of other societies, and in any case, there is a marked overlap between this category and some others, such as the apotropaic or Dionysiac material. We can, however, be certain that some of the objects which in modern times have seemed shocking or embarrassing would have appeared merely amusing to their users in antiquity. The final category is the important one of imagery which is definitely and primarily erotic, and was intended to be sexually stimulating to those who saw it. This group of illustrations is most common on decorated pottery, both Greek and Roman, and concentrates on scenes of actual copulation. It is this material alone which should be classified as 'erotic'; all the other classes are intended for other purposes.

In recent times, all the ancient material which has seemed openly sexual has been regarded as obscene; not only that which depicts scenes of lovemaking, but also representations of genitals made as amulets or medical *ex votos*, or pictures of sexually aroused mythical satyrs at their Dionysiac revels. Definitions of obscenity remain an unsolved problem, but many legal definitions include the concept of 'depraving and corrupting' the viewer, rather than merely arousing him or her sexually. It is extremely difficult to see how representations of the nude human body can possibly deprave and corrupt, or indeed how illustrations of sexual intercourse can do so, since the usual heterosexual form of this is a normal activity, and moreover essential to the continuance of the species. If it is thought that sexual activity which cannot result in offspring is immoral, then a picture of homosexual connection or coitus with an animal might just possibly be said to corrupt, provided the onlooker had been too unimaginative to envisage the activity for himself, surely a very rare case. It is in any case clear that the Victorians, and many people at the present day, do not confine their condemnation to such scenes alone, but apparently consider sexual excitement as wrong in itself, so that everything which may be conducive to it, or relate to it in some way, is suspect.

This brings us to the whole question of ways of looking at the past. Should we, in fact, interpret antiquity in terms of our own cultural conditioning, or should we make some attempt to be more objective? The paintings on Greek pottery and the bronze pendants made in the Roman Empire were not made with us in mind. What can we possibly learn about the past if we insist on studying it only in terms of our own reactions? The answer, surely, is nothing. We must therefore make an effort to see all archaeological material as far as we can in terms of its own time; our personal reactions to the material are irrelevant if our purpose is to try to understand an ancient society. This is not easy, but that scarcely constitutes an excuse for not trying to do it. In the nineteenth century, the study of the past was often used as a basis for systems of moral ideology, and was considered useful for demonstrating the consequences of wrong behaviour. While it is certainly true that much can be learned from the study of history, we do not see it in quite these terms now. The hypocrisy of avoiding study of sexual customs can very easily be illustrated by the attitude, both now and in the past, to the study of certain other social customs in antiquity. It is no longer thought acceptable to indulge in forms of 'sport' which have as their ultimate aim the slaughter of the losing human

119 A Roman lamp decorated with a
winged phallus. Late 1st century BC

contestant, yet we accept that Roman society cannot be fully understood if the sports of the arena are ignored, and students of the period have seemed to have no difficulty in tolerating discussion and illustration of material relating to this, however much they may deprecate it in moral terms.

The first problem in the study of the past therefore reveals itself as deliberate bias on the part of the student himself. It should be possible to set this aside as soon as one is conscious of it. Some, however, might argue that, however desirable an objective approach might be, we already have a great deal of evidence about life in antiquity, and we will not greatly distort the picture if we suppress one category of evidence, that relating to sexuality, because it is embarrassing or distasteful to us. A little thought will demonstrate that this attitude is totally false: we have to look at the nature and the built-in biases and gaps in the data on which we base our interpretation of antiquity, and this will prove that we are very far indeed from having a wide or balanced range of information.

The evidence for vanished societies consists of two main classes, written and material. Written sources may be consciously historical, or they may have been written for literary or quite mundane everyday purposes, and they can be written from within the society in question or from outside it. The material, or archaeological, evidence consists of the structures built by the people and the objects used by them, and of their remains. In studying prehistory, only the latter form of evidence is available. Classical antiquity can be seen through a combination of written and archaeological sources, but the biases of both these types of evidence are greater and more basic than many people realise.

We have already commented on conscious and deliberate bias in the student. There is also much unconscious bias. Even without making indignant moral value-judgements, based on the belief that our society is right and others wrong, we can still misunderstand the atmosphere and feeling of another culture. One of the most obvious aspects of this is in the matter of language. Anyone who is bi-lingual, or who even speaks more than one language with a fair degree of fluency, will know that their actual modes of thought are affected by the language in which they are thinking and speaking at any given moment. The syntax and vocabulary tend to impose certain types of thought-processes. The differences are evident even in closely related modern European languages, and are correspondingly more marked in those of different families and periods. In the case of modern languages, the barriers can be crossed by the individual whose command of the language is sufficiently good, partly because the culture which surrounds that language is still extant, but it is doubtful whether even the most technically brilliant classical scholar could totally overcome the problem with ancient Greek and Latin. Victorian classicists, enviably fluent as many of them were in Greek especially, infatuated by Greek culture and deeply read in its literature, were still able to misunderstand and distort the values of the ancient world. Unconscious bias is also present in the whole area of personal cultural conditioning. Our own society's norms can so easily appear universal if we are not prepared to examine them sharply when dealing with other cultures.

The internal biases of the student of the past, conscious and otherwise, are equalled by those of the data which he studies. It may be thought that historical sources are reliable and helpful, but this is not necessarily so. Our present concept of both the writing and interpretation of history is, with a few exceptions, not very old. Though the idea that the raw material should consist of facts, arranged in a

120 A crater by the Pan Painter, decorated with a woman carrying a huge model phallus, probably in connection with some festival. Second quarter of the 5th century BC

logical manner, goes back to the Greek historian Thucydides, there have been many historians of a very different stamp in the meantime. English, a language with many shades of meaning in its vocabulary, has a distinction between the words 'history' and 'story', but many related modern European languages do not: *histoire* in French, *Geschichte* in German, *storia* in Italian and *hanes* in Welsh all mean 'tale', and often specifically an unlikely tale, as well as 'history'. Though by the nineteenth century it was not acceptable, let alone praiseworthy, to 'improve' a story of some historical event by embellishing it in a colourful and memorable way, it was certainly still acceptable to suppress information which was considered distasteful and, above all, to approve or condemn the event in terms of contemporary, nineteenth-century morality. History had to make sense as a story written by a nineteenth-century Christian. This is one of the reasons why Richard Payne Knight's sincere attempts to study the religious symbolism of sexual imagery in antiquity met with such savage condemnation.

The readers of historical sources may therefore have many forms of bias to contend with, where the writers have consciously or unconsciously distorted their material. If purposely writing history, the author may have indulged in deliberate propaganda. This is often easy enough for the reader to detect and allow for even centuries later, but sometimes it can be subtle and highly effective. There are many who believe, for example, that the 'bad press' received by King Richard III of England gives a totally false picture of his life and reign which has been uncritically accepted ever since. The usual version of his career was certainly a convenient one for the Tudor monarchs who succeeded him.

Deliberate distortion by writers of history may be for literary reasons rather than political ones; this is perhaps truer of the medieval period than the classical. Roman writers were conscious of writing history in more or less our sense of the word – though they were not objective, for reasons we shall see in a moment – but medieval historians such as Geoffrey of Monmouth were concerned to produce an entertaining and plausible story. Geoffrey, who lived in the twelfth century, wrote a *History of the Kings of Britain*, allegedly based on an older Welsh manuscript, which is a fine and stirring piece of work from the literary standpoint, embellishing a tiny kernel of fact with a vivid shell of conjecture and imagination. He was the source of much detail about the Arthurian legend, and was long taken as a reasonably reliable guide to the early history of Britain.

Another bias of written history concerns the cultural viewpoint of the writer. We have several important texts on the events of the first centuries BC and AD which eventually led to the absorption of Britain into the Roman Empire, and these are rightly regarded as extremely valuable sources. Nevertheless, we must remember that all of them were written by the conquering Romans, not by the conquered British Celts. While the facts may be correct, we can be certain that some other material would emerge in a history written from the other side. These histories, like most of those written with posterity in mind, also contain another bias; they deal with the important, large movements of events – military and political activities, the doings of kings, statesmen and generals. Any understanding of history must, of course, involve these matters, but the modern student of the past also wants to know about ordinary people and everyday life. These were matters which were too well known, and perhaps too uninteresting, to contemporaries to be included in historical writing. Facts about trade, commerce and other aspects of economic life are likewise often absent from

121 A vase by the
Perseus Painter,
showing a herm with a
bird perching on his
phallus, and an altar.
Second quarter of the
5th century BC

122 *above* Roman *spintriae*, coin-like tokens with erotic scenes on one face.

123 A Roman wall-carving of a winged phallus and an Evil Eye, from Leptis Magna in Libya.

sources written as history, though they are now of great interest to us.

All these problems may cause one to turn hopefully from written history to the apparently impartial data provided by archaeological methods. At least these deal primarily with everyday life, and presumably nobody in the past thought how they might mislead an archaeologist of the future. Archaeology is not, however, a discipline based on complete and unbiased evidence: far from it. The structures and portable objects which survive from the past for us to assess and study form only a small proportion of the material culture of the past, and we have available to us only a tiny proportion, in turn, of what originally survived: much has been destroyed in the intervening centuries, and much has not yet been found.

Furthermore, the survival of objects is extremely unbalanced. A glance at the illustrations in this book will demonstrate how common pottery artefacts are compared with many other classes of material. Fired clay is a substance which survives exceptionally well; though it breaks, it seldom decomposes. It was used in huge quantities in many early societies, being cheap, fragile and easily replaceable, and consequently there is still a lot of it around. The study of it can therefore be more broadly based than that of many other types of artefact. Metals and glass, for instance, can be reused by actually reprocessing them, while most organic materials simply do not survive in reasonable condition for centuries on end. Our comparatively poor knowledge of the range of utensils made of wood, cloth, bone, leather and basketwork in ancient times contrasts markedly with the minuteness with which we can chronicle changes of style in the pottery.

Our judgement of an ancient society's artistic achievement is also dependent on whether they chose to express their creativity in relatively durable media. On the whole, stone sculpture survives well, though marble can be burnt to produce lime for mortar, a fate which befell much classical sculpture. Large-scale bronze statues could be melted down and the metal used for other purposes, though given some good luck, they are capable of surviving the centuries. Paintings have scarcely survived at all from antiquity; though we admire the wall-paintings which have come down to us, such as those from Pompeii, they were not classed in their own time as great art. Much of our judgement of Greek and Roman art is based on *Kleinkunst* – decorated silverware, painted pottery, small statuettes, jewellery, and so on: perfectly valid subjects for study, but presenting only part of the picture. Ancient societies whose artistic endeavours reached their finest flowering in some more perishable form, such as woodcarving or decorated textiles, have left little behind them for us to admire.

All in all, though the gaps and biases of archaeological sources are quite different from those of written history, they are just as glaring, and they make it extraordinarily difficult for us to gain a well-rounded picture of the society which they represent. The interpretation of archaeological data is often a matter of opinion, and surprisingly divergent theories can be put forward to explain the same set of facts. There is little point in amassing information about the past unless some attempt is made to organise it into a coherent picture, but there are changing fashions in styles of interpretation and in the subjects of greatest interest, so that models of the past are continually being revised or overthrown. At present, the art-historical and typological approaches are thought *passé* by many, while more 'scientific' and mathematical approaches are popular. The old-fashioned technique of explaining earlier societies, particularly prehistoric ones, by means of anthropological parallels remains very acceptable in some circles. All these approaches are valid in certain respects, and have drawbacks in others.

If we accept, firstly, that our study of the past should be as objective as we can make it, and secondly, that the sources available to us are both incomplete and intrinsically biased, it must surely become clear that the deliberate suppression of any type of evidence is extremely serious. Material of the Greek and Roman period which was earlier set aside because it was judged obscene is quite common (exactly how common is not easy to establish, precisely because of the separate treatment it has been accorded), and any earnest research into the world of Greece and Rome must include it. If one wishes to draw conclusions from any group of facts, it should be obvious that it is hardly wise to begin by arbitrarily ignoring part of the evidence.

Other than this point, which is one of commonsense as much as scholarly integrity, what point is there in trying to understand and interpret the sexual imagery in Greek and Roman visual art? Perhaps the most striking is the insight which it affords into the contrast between our attitudes and those of antiquity, even though many of us consider ourselves free of the puritanical feelings of the previous century. This is a very clear reminder that we are different in a great many ways from the people of the classical cultures, and our awareness of this should help us understand them more fully, by making us examine our own assumptions and preconceptions constantly.

The relationship of sexual imagery to religious belief and practice is also absolutely central, and religious feeling is always a key aspect of a society. Man has always been anxious to concentrate on the features of his species which distinguish him from other animals, and has therefore had rather complex feelings about those aspects of behaviour which he shares with the rest of the animal kingdom. This was true in classical antiquity, but sexuality was not denied or considered damaging to spiritual growth as it has been in so many Christian societies. It was instead channelled into acceptable forms of expression, and treated with humour and commonsense.

The evidence for sexual attitudes in the visual arts is illuminating to those who study these societies mainly through the literary evidence. The two types of data may not always seem to support each other: as we have seen, in the case of the Greek attitude to homosexuality, the combined written and visual evidence provides many answers, but it also poses some questions. The position of the two sexes in society is naturally evident in sources of different kinds, and the artistic imagery specifically concerned with sexual matters can be of great interest. We have to allow for the fact that most of the artists and craftsmen were probably male, but even so, something of the place of women in society must come through.

Finally, the exclusion of 'improper' artefacts from general studies of antiquity means that some very fine artistic evidence as such is being ignored. The illustrations in the previous chapters should give some idea of the quality of much of this material in artistic terms: some of the work on Greek painted pottery and on Roman ceramics such as Arretine ware is among the best of its kind. For this reason alone, it is necessary to bring these objects back into proper consideration with their fellows, instead of pretending that they do not exist.

Many of us, more honest than some of our predecessors, will also admit to a natural interest in sexual matters, and will regard this, too, as a sufficient reason to examine all the evidence possible which refers to the subject in antiquity. A dislike of hypocrisy is itself enough to condemn the attitude which tries to keep the material hidden. But there are real academic advantages to be gained from bringing it out into the open from the secret collections to which it was relegated by earlier workers. We can learn much not only about the ancient societies which were so important for the growth of European culture, but also about the basic principles of the study of the past and the way in which they are changing and developing. In short, a good look at the sexual images of Greece and Rome can teach us a great deal about people, past and present.

124 A red-figure jug by the Shuvalov Painter, with a very young couple. Last quarter of the 5th century BC

Sources
of illustrations

The photographs were obtained by the institutions which own the objects, except where indicated. The author and publishers are grateful to the copyright holders for permission to reproduce the photographs.

Black and white

1. Photo Peter Clayton
2. London, British Museum (G & R): Vase E 76
3. Photo Philip Kenrick
4. Naples, National Museum: RP 27695 (photo Fabrizio Parisio)
7. London, British Museum (M & LA)
8. London, British Museum (M & LA)
9. London, British Museum (G & R): Vase F 65
11. London, British Museum (M & LA): M 560, 562
12. London, British Museum (G & R): 1824.4-47.1
13. London, British Museum (G & R): 1865.11-18.40 (W 40)
14. Naples, National Museum: RP 129477 (photo Fabrizio Parisio)
15. London, British Museum (G & R): 1912.11-25
16. Oxford, Ashmolean Museum: 1966.252
17. Museum of London
18. London, British Museum (G & R): Q 761
19. London, British Museum (G & R): Q 882
20, 21. Photos Ronald Sheridan's Photo Library
22. London, British Museum (G & R): 1824.4-71.4
23. Drawing by Catherine Johns
24. Naples, National Museum (photo Ronald Sheridan's Photo Library)
25. London, British Museum (P & RB): P.1981.11-2.1
26. Berlin (E), Staatliche Museen zu Berlin: F 2275
27. Rome, Villa Giulia
28. London, British Museum (G & R): Vase E 65
29. Museum of London: A.21474
30. London, British Museum (P & RB): 1946.10-7.1
31. Naples, National Museum: RP 27710 (photo Fabrizio Parisio)
32. Naples, National Museum: RP 27732 (photo Fabrizio Parisio)
33. Naples, National Museum: RP 27717 (photo Fabrizio Parisio)
34. Naples, National Museum: RP 27732 (photo Fabrizio Parisio)
35. Boston, Museum of Fine Arts (Gift of E.P. Warren): Res. 08.32p
36. Copenhagen, Nationalmuseet, Antiksamlingen: 119 (photo Lennart Larsen)
37. Naples, National Museum: PR 129434 (photo Fabrizio Parisio)
38. Boston, Museum of Fine Arts (Pierce Fund): 04.24
39. Naples, National Museum: RP 27854 (photo Fabrizio Parisio)
40. Photo Ronald Sheridan's Photo Library

41–44. London, British Museum (G & R): 1756.1-1.1007, 1839.1-4.254, 1865.11-18.104, 119
45. London, British Museum (G & R): M 516
46. Photo Catherine Johns
47. Naples, National Museum: RP 27741 (photo Fabrizio Parisio)
48. London, British Museum (P & RB)
49. London, British Museum (G & R): 1888.6-1.496C
50. Paris, Musée du Louvre: 307 (photo by Photographie Bulloz)
51. London, British Museum (G & R): 1865.11-18.78
52. Trier, Rheinisches Landesmuseum: G 92
53. London, British Museum (G & R): 1824.4-32.2
54. Naples, National Museum: RP 27855 (photo Fabrizio Parisio)
55. Boston, Museum of Fine Arts (Donated by E.P. Warren): Res. 08.320
56. London, British Museum (G & R): 1974.7-5.1
57. London, British Museum (G & R): 1977.1-7.1
58. London, British Museum (G & R): Q 1025
59. York, Yorkshire Museum
60. Photo Ronald Sheridan's Photo Library
61. London, British Museum (M & LA): 1958.12-2.1
62. Munich, Staatliche Antikensammlung: 2044
63. London, British Museum (G & R): B 300
64. Boston, Museum of Fine Arts (Gift of London T. Clay): 68.163
65. See 31
66. Munich, Staatliche Antikensammlung: 1432
67. Naples, National Museum: RP 27669 (photo Fabrizio Parisio)
68. London, British Museum (P & RB): P.1981.2-1
69. Munich, Staatliche Antikensammlung: 2657
70. Photo Ronald Sheridan's Photo Library
71. Berlin (W), Antikenmuseum, Staatliche Museen Preuissischer Kulturbesitz: 1964.4 (photo Jutta Tietz-Glagow)
72. Berlin (E), Staatliche Museen zu Berlin: F 1671
73. Boston, Museum of Fine Arts (Gift of E.P. Warren): 10.651
74. London, British Museum (G & R): Terracotta 1676
75. Naples, National Museum: RP 27859 (photo Fabrizio Parisio)
76. Oxford, Ashmolean Museum
77. Photo Paul Arthur
78. Cambridge, University Museum of Archaeology and Anthropology: 81-320
79. London, British Museum (P & RB): 1857.8-6.1

80. Peterborough, City Museum & Art Gallery: L59/66
(photo Peterborough City Council)

81. Oxford, Ashmolean Museum: 1967.304

82. Berlin (W), Antikenmuseum, Staatliche Museen Preuissischer Kulturbesitz: F 2279
(photo Jutta Tietz-Glagow)

83. Munich, Staatliche Antikensammlung: 1468

84. Oxford, Ashmolean Museum

85. Paris, Musée du Louvre: MA 231
(photo Chuzeville)

86. London, British Museum (P & RB): 1848.8-3.44

87. Boston, Museum of Fine Arts (Gift of E.P. Warren): Res. 80.34c

88. London, British Museum (G & R): Q 871

89. Athens, American School of Classical Studies in Athens, Agora Excavations: L 519

90. London, British Museum (G & R): 1971.4-26.39

91. London, British Museum (G & R): Q 900

92. Naples, National Museum: RP 27669
(photo Fabrizio Parisio)

93. Florence, Archaeological Museum: 3921
(photo Soprintendentza alle Antichità – Firenze)

94. London, British Museum (G & R): Gem no. 555

95. Boston, Museum of Fine Arts (Gift of E.P. Warren): Res. 08.32c

96. London, British Museum (G & R): Q 916

97. Boston, Museum of Fine Arts: 95.61

98. London, British Museum (G & R): D 213

99. London, British Museum (G & R): 1865.11-18.40

100. St. Germaine-en-Laye, Musée Nationale des Antiquités: inv. 72474

101, 102. Oxford, Ashmolean Museum: 1966.252

103. Drawing Catherine Johns

104. Princeton, Art Museum: 56.104

105, 106. Tarquinia, City Museum

107. Paris, Musée du Louvre: G 13
(photo Chuzeville)

108. Florence, Archaeological Museum: 3921
(photo Soprintendenza alle Antichità – Firenze)

109. Oxford, Ashmolean Museum: 1967.305

110. Paris, Musée du Louvre: C 9682
(photo Chuzeville)

111. Boston, Museum of Fine Arts: 1970.233

112. Boston, Museum of Fine Arts: Res.

113. London, British Museum (G & R): 08.32c 1855.12-26.874

114. See 15

115. Naples, National Museum: RP 27864
(photo Fabrizio Parisio)

116. Nicosia, Cyprus Museum: D 2759

117. Berlin (W), Antikenmuseum, Staatliche Museen Preussischer Kulturbesitz: 3251
(photo Jutta Tietz-Glagow)

118. London, British Museum (P & RB)

119. London, British Museum (G & R): Q 720

120. Berlin (E), Staatliche Museen zu Berlin: 3206

121. Berlin (W), Antikenmuseum, Staatliche Museen Preussischer Kulturbesitz: F 2172
(photo Jutta Tietz-Glagow)

122. Oxford, Ashmolean Museum

123. Photo Philip Kenrick

124. Berlin (W), Antikenmuseum, Staatliche Museen Preussischer Kulturbesitz: F 2412
(photo Jutta Tietz-Glagow)

pp. 114–5 Brussels, Musées Royaux d'Art et d'Histoire: R 351

p. 116 Rome, Capitoline Museum
(photo Barbara Malter)

Back Cover Rome, Capitoline Museum: 408
(photo Barbara Malter)

Colour

1. Naples, National Museum: RP 27709
(photo Antonia Mulas)

2. Photo Antonia Mulas

3. London, British Museum (G & R): Vase E 76

4. Naples, National Museum: RP 27714
(photo Antonia Mulas)

5. London, British Museum (G & R): E 810

6. Photo Antonia Mulas

7. Naples, National Museum: RP
(photo Fabrizio Parisio)

8. Naples, National Museum: RP 2770
(photo Antonia Mulas)

9. London, British Museum (G & R): C 528

10. London, British Museum (G & R):
Marshall 2958, 2959, 2961, 2963, 2964, 3133; 1772.3-14.24, 34; 1872.6-4.340, 341

11. Vienna, Kunsthistorisches Museum: IX B 1560
(photo by Photo Meyer)

12. Photo Catherine Johns

13. London, British Museum (G & R): 1856.12-26.1086

14. Naples, National Museum: PR 27853
(photo Antonia Mulas)

15. Boston, Museum of Fine Arts: 08.34d
(photo Antonia Mulas)

16. London, British Museum (P & RB): 1946.10-7.1

17. Thessalonike, Archaeological Museum: Derveni B 1

18. Athens, National Museum: 3728
(photo Antonia Mulas)

19. Photo by Scala, Florence

20. Munich, Staatliche Antikensammlung: 2654
(photo Caecilia Moessner)

21. London, British Museum (G & R): 2199

22. Naples, National Museum: RP 6713
(photo Antonia Mulas)

23. Naples, National Museum
(photo Antonia Mulas)

24. Photo by Scala, Florence

25. Oxford, Ashmolean Museum

26, 27. London, British Museum (G & R): 1865.11-18.43, 39

28. Boston, Museum of Fine Arts: 08.292
(photo Antonia Mulas)

29. Photo Ronald Sheridan Photo Library

30. Oxford, Ashmolean Museum

31. Brussels, Musées Royaux d'Art et d'Histoire: R.351
(photo Sergio Purin)

32. Naples, National Museum: RC 144
(photo Antonia Mulas)

33. London, British Museum (G & R): 1865.11-18.44

34. Berlin (W), Antikenmuseum Staatliche Museen Preussischer Kulturbesitz: 2412
(photo Bildarchiv Preussischer Kulturbesitz)

35. Rome, Capitoline Museum
(photo Antonia Mulas)

36. Naples, National Museum: RP 27714
(photo Antonia Mulas)

37. Naples, National Museum: RP
(photo Fabrizio Parisio)

38. Naples, National Museum: RP 27697
(photo Antonia Mulas)

Front Cover see 30

Bibliography

A full bibliography of the books and articles which have contributed in some way to the facts and ideas presented in this book would be inappropriate and tediously long, ranging as it would from standard reference works to articles on individual objects, and from archaeology and art-history to sexology and pornography. It therefore seemed sensible to list only a very brief selection of the works which are most directly concerned with the argument of the book, or are actually referred to in the text.

BIEBER, Margarete, *The History of the Greek and Roman Theatre* (Princeton University Press, 1961)

BOARDMAN, John, *Athenian Black-figure Vases* (Thames and Hudson, London, 1974)

BOARDMAN, John, *Athenian Red-figure Vases: the Archaic Period* (Thames & Hudson, London, 1975)

BOARDMAN, John, *Eros in Greece* (John Murray, London, 1978)

BOWIE, Theodore, & CHRISTENSON, Cornelia V., *Studies in Erotic Art* (Basic Books, New York, 1970)

BRENDEL, Otto, *The Scope and Temperament of Erotic Art in the Greco-Roman World* (in Bowie & Christenson, *op. cit.*)

DOVER, Kenneth J., *Greek Homosexuality* (Duckworth, London, 1978)

EDWARDS, Edward, *Lives of the Founders of the British Museum* (London, 1870)

GRANT, Michael, *Erotic Art in Pompeii* (Octopus, London, 1975)

HARRISON, Fraser, *The Dark Angel: Aspects of Victorian Sexuality* (Sheldon Press, London, 1077; Fontana, 1979)

JENKYNS, Richard, *The Victorians and Ancient Greece* (Blackwell, Oxford, 1980)

KIEFER, Otto, *Sexual Life in Ancient Rome* (Abbey Library, London, 1934)

KNIGHT, Richard Payne, *A Discourse on the Worship of Priapus* (London, 1786)

LEWINSOHN, Richard, *Eine Weltgeschichte der Sexualität* (Rowohlt Verlag, Hamburg, 1956)

LICHT, Hans, *Sexual Life in Ancient Greece* (Abbey Library, London, 1932, translated from *Sittengeschichte Griechenlands*, Dresden, 1925/6)

LO DUCA, J-M., *Histoire de l'Érotisme* (La Jeune Parque, Paris, 1969)

LUCIE-SMITH, Edward, *Eroticism in Western Art* (Thames & Hudson, London, 1972)

MELVILLE, Robert, *Erotic Art of the West* (Wiedenfeld & Nicholson, London, 1973)

MORRIS, D., Collett, P., Marsh, P., O'Shaughessy, M., *Gestures* (Jonathan Cape, London, 1979)

PEARSALL, Ronald, *The Worm in the Bud: the world of Victorian Sexuality* (Weidenfeld & Nicholson, London, 1969; Pelican 1971)

PERRIN, Noel, *Dr Bowdler's Legacy* (Macmillan, London, 1970)

POMEROY, Sarah B., *Goddesses, Whores, Wives and Slaves: women in Classical Antiquity* (Schocken Books, New York, 1975)

POTTER, T.W., 'A Republican healing-sanctuary at Ponte di Nona near Rome and the Classical Tradition of Votive Medicine', *Antiquaries Journal* (forthcoming)

SCOTT, George Ryley, *Phallic Worship* (Luxor Press, London, 1966)

SELTMAN, Charles, *Women in Antiquity* (Thames & Hudson, London, 1956)

SIMONS, G.L., *Sex and Superstition* (Abelard-Schumann, London, 1973)

TANNAHILL, Reay, *Sex in History* (Hamish Hamilton, London, 1980)

TRUDGILL, Eric, *Madonnas and Magdalens* (Heinemann, London, 1976)

TURNBULL, Percival, 'The Phallus in the Art of Roman Britain', *Bulletin of the Institute of Archaeology* 15 (1978), 199

VORBERG, Gaston, *Glossarium Eroticum* (Original edn 1932, reprinted Hanau 1965)

WEBB, Peter (ed), *The Erotic Arts* (Secker & Warburg, 1975)

WILSON, Simon, *Short History of Western Erotic Art* (in Melville, *op. cit.*)

YOUNG, Wayland, *Eros Denied* (Weidenfeld & Nicholson, London, 1964)

Index

The figures in ordinary type refer to page numbers. Figures in *italic* refer to black and white illustrations, and those in **bold** to the colour illustrations.

Achilles 85
Actors 87–8
Adriatic Sea 117
Agave 78
Alkibiades 52
Altamira, Spain *21*
Amphitheatre *see* Games, Roman
Amulets 62, 63, 64, 72, 73, 74, 75, 143, 144
Anal intercourse 101, 102, 133, 134
Animals 39, 40, 42, 54, 57, 59, 68, 80, 86, 106–113
Antefixes 74–75; *59*
Anthesteria 85, 86
Antinous 102
Antiquaries, Society of 22
Antlered god 64
Aphrodite 41, 54, 104; *see also* Venus
Apollo 41, 56
Apuleius, Lucius *The Golden Ass* 111
Archon 86
Aretino, Pietro 21
Aristophanes 86, 89–90, 102
Arnobius 50
Arretine ware 33, 52, 102, 124–127, 136, 137, 142, 152; *16, 38, 101, 102*; **30**
Artemis 41; *24*
Asclepius 56; *40*
Ashbee, Henry Spencer 28
Asses *see* Donkeys
Athens 9, 42, 52, 86, 89, 90
   theatre of Dionysos *60*
Augustus 124

Bacchanalia 85
Bacchantes *see* Maenads
Bacchus 56, 85, *65*; *see also* Dionysos
Bath, City of 56
Bath-houses 64
Baubo 75
Beads 66
Bells 67–68, 70; *39, 52, 54*; **13, 14**
Berlin 127
Bestiality 106–113, 118, 119, 144; *90, 91, 92*
Bible 17, 41
Birdoswald, Roman fort 63, 64
Birds 70, 108, 113; *121*
   Phallus-birds 50, 53
Bison *21*
Blindness 66
Boars 63, 64
Boccaccio, *The Decameron* 19
Bona Dea 50
Bordeaux 123
Boston 72, 135
Boundary-markers 42, 52
British Library, Private Case 30
British Museum 22, 24, 25, 28, 29–30, 31, 32, 66
Browning, Robert, *Pippa Passes* 17
Buffalo 39
Bulls 64, 86, 110; *see also* Cattle

Caduceus 54, 70
Carrum navale see Ship-cart
Castor 107
Cats 70
Cattle 39; *see also* Bulls
Celts 35, 41, 50, 54, 56, 63, 64, 66, 72, 75, 117, 119, 148
Centaurs 84–85, 107; *77*
Ceres *see* Demeter
Cerne Abbas, hill-figure *20*
Cernunnos 64
Chariot-racing *see* Games, Roman
Chesters, Roman fort 64
Chiron 85
Choes 86
Cholera 28
Choregoi 86
Chorus 86, 87, 90
Christianity 9, 25–26, 40, 45, 50, 56, 62, 63, 78, 85, 101, 102, 113, 148, 152
Circus *see* Games, Roman
Claudius 32
Clitoris 72
Cockerels 54, 101; *94*
Coins 22
Coitus, positions for 129–137
Colchester 79
Contraception 134
Corinth 41; *112*
Cornucopia 40, 41
Cosimo, Saint 24
Crete 110
Crocodile 91
Cunnilingus 141; *116*
Cupid *see* Eros
Cyprus 41

Damian, St 24
Deer 64, 82, 84, 101, 106; *45*; **26, 27**
Delos *1*
Demeter 41
Demetrios, Ephesian silversmith 41
Devil 45
Dherveni, Macedonia *17*
Diana *see* Artemis
Dildo 91, 102, 142; *97*
Dilettanti, Society of 22, 25
Dionysia 85–86
Dionysos 10, 42, 44, 50, 56, 78–81, 84, 85, 86, 90, 119, 143, 144; *60, 62, 63, 64*; **9**
Discourse on the Worship of Priapus 21, 22–28; *5, 10*
Dithyramb 86
Dogs 40, 50, 66, 68, 70, 110, 123, 134; *100*; **35**
Dolphins 66, 79; *62*
Domitian 33
Donkeys 84, 110, 111, 113
Dover, Sir Kenneth 101, 103, 133
Drama 10, 56, 78, 85, 86, 87–91, 142, 143; *see also* Satyr-plays
Drunkenness 81, 84, 119, 142; *65*
Dunbar, William 18
Dwarfs 118–119; *96*

Eagle 110
Ecstasy, Bacchic 78, 80
Edwards, Edward, *Lives of the Founders of the British Museum* 26
Egypt 75